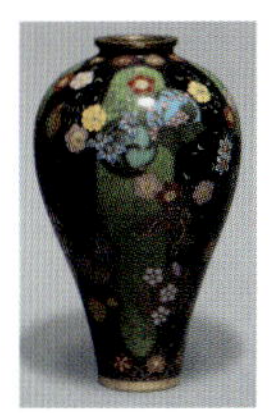

JAPANESE CLOISONNÉ ENAMELS

The Seven Treasures

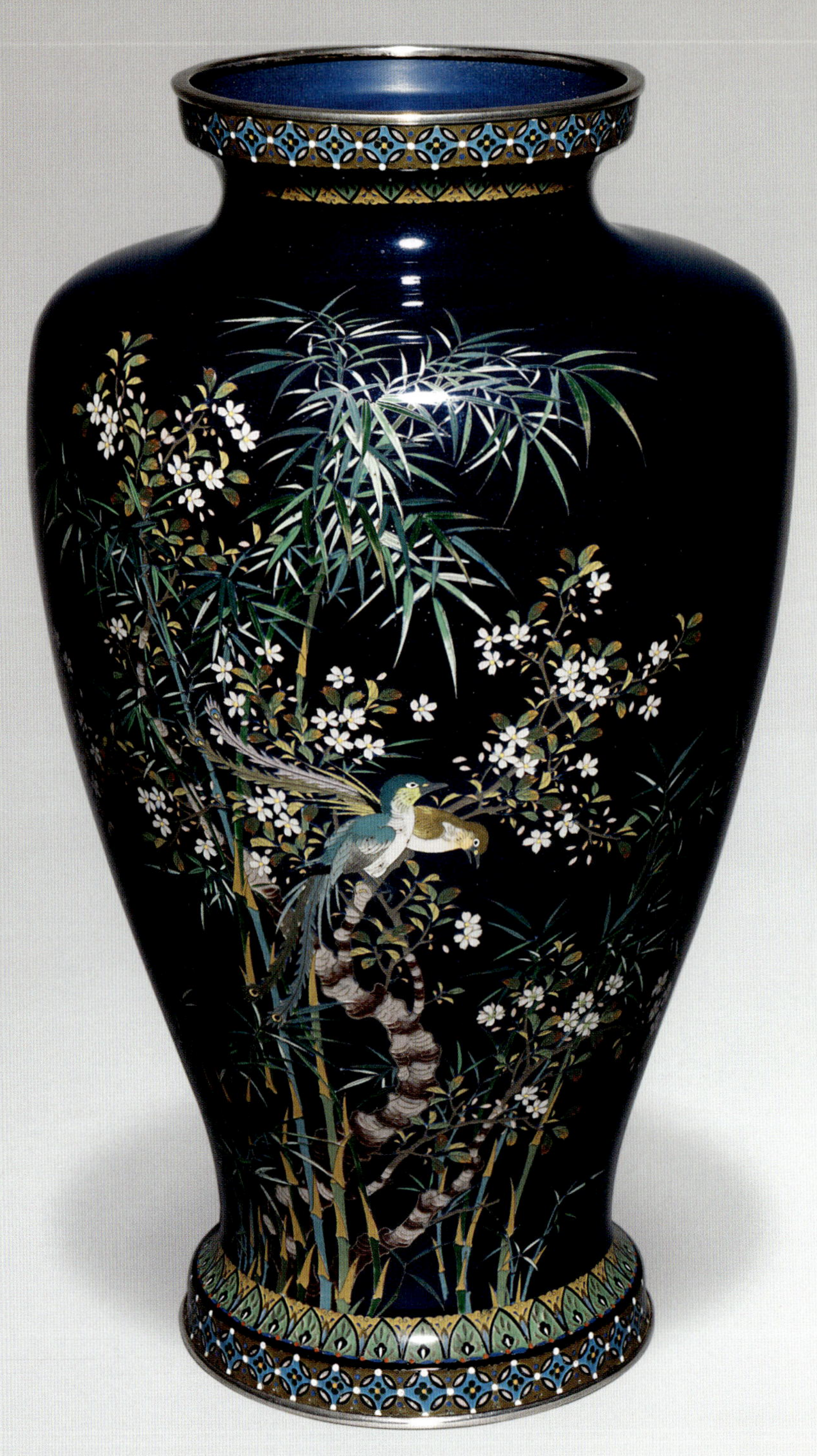

JAPANESE CLOISONNÉ ENAMELS

The Seven Treasures

Gregory Irvine

V&A Publishing

First published by V&A Publishing, 2011
V&A Publishing
Victoria and Albert Museum
South Kensington
London SW7 2RL

Paperback edition

ISBN 978 1 85177 657 3

10 9 8 7 6 5 4 3 2 1
2015 2014 2013 2012 2011

Designer: Andrew Shoolbred
Copy-editor: Caroline Brooke Johnson
New photography by Ian Thomas,
V&A Photography by V&A Photographic Studio

Front cover illustration: Vase (plate 69)
Back cover illustration: Group of lidded vases (plate 33)
Frontispiece: Vase (plate 23)
Half-title illustration: Vase (plate 29)

Printed in Hong Kong

V&A Publishing

Supporting the world's leading
museum of art and design,
the Victoria and Albert
Museum, London

CONTENTS

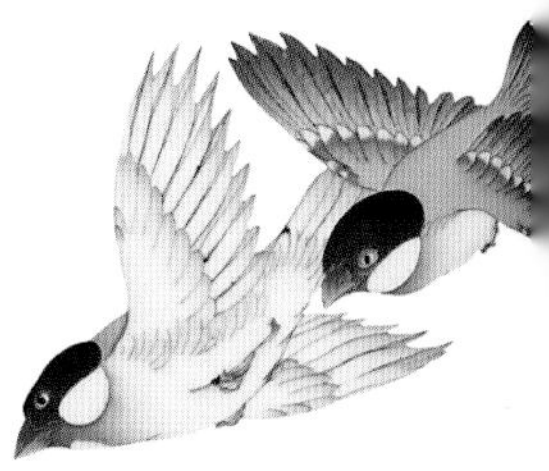

FOREWORD

This book has been made possible through the continuing generosity of Mr Edwin Davies, OBE, who has for many years been one of the Victoria and Albert Museum's most generous and philanthropic benefactors. Mr Davies has built up a fine collection of Japanese cloisonné enamels, mostly from what is known as the 'Golden Age' (*c.*1880–1910). The V&A's existing collections, while strong in earlier works and in cloisonné-decorated sword fittings was singularly deficient in almost any objects from this period. In 2010 Mr Davies generously offered the V&A a substantial part of his collection, which now enables us to present a far more rounded picture of one of Japan's most exquisite art forms.

As well as expressing my deepest thanks to Mr Davies, I would also like to thank at the V&A, Ian Thomas, the photographer who has so expertly captured the beauty of these objects and Emmie Ratter who has patiently helped me with many aspects of this book. Thanks also to Malcolm Fairley and the late Dr Oliver Impey who have both shared their extensive knowledge with me over the years, and to the many museum colleagues in the UK and particularly in Japan with whom I have had the pleasure to share both knowledge and enthusiasm for this superb form of craftsmanship.

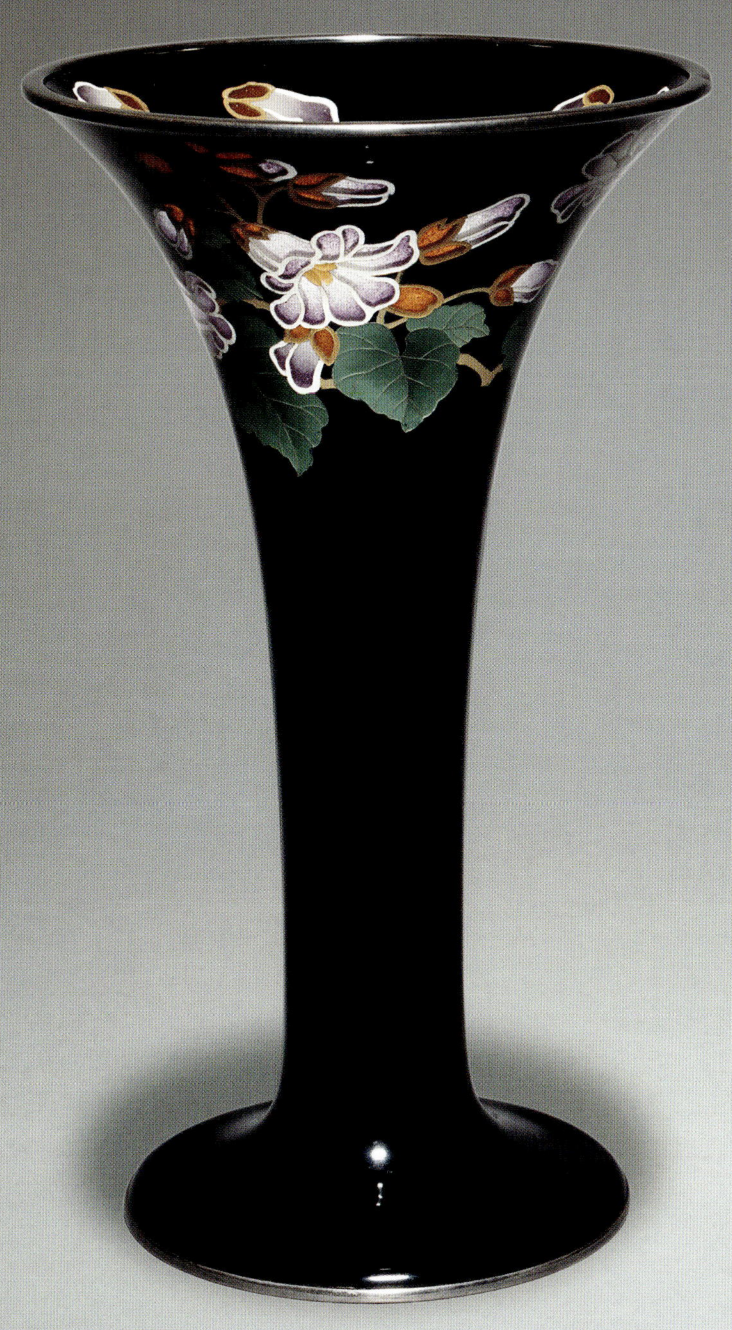

INTRODUCTION

There are two distinct qualities or types expressed in Japanese art: one suggesting endless patience in the execution of minute detail, the other denoting a momentary conception of some fleeting idea carried out with boldness and freedom of expression in form and line – profuse complexity and extreme simplicity… the work on Japanese cloisonné ware generally exhibits the quality suggestive of unwearying labour and patience. (Harada 1911, p.271)

The characters for the word *shippo*, the Japanese term for enamels, mean 'Seven Treasures', which is a reference to the Seven Treasures mentioned in Buddhist texts. Although these treasures may vary, they generally include the following: gold, silver, emerald, coral, agate, lapis lazuli and pearl. The Japanese applied this term to the rich colours found on Chinese enamel wares and to those that they later made themselves.

Enamels are a form of glass coloured with metallic oxides and applied as a paste, usually to a metallic body which, when fired in a kiln, melts and fuses to the body; when cool, the surface of the object is polished to a high-gloss finish. The simplest form of enamelling is *champlevé*, whereby a design is carved out of a metallic body, the enamel paste is applied into the resulting hollow and the piece is fired and polished. In cloisonné enamelling fine wires are used to delineate areas (*cloisons* in French, hence *cloisonné*) into which the enamel paste is applied. These wires serve a dual function: they can be an integral part of the decoration and can also prevent molten enamels from flowing into adjoining areas of the design.

Enamels require a body, generally of copper (although silver and ceramic can be used) onto which a design is first drawn in ink. Fine wires, made usually of brass and at times of varying thickness, are then bent and hammered into the required shape and carefully glued along the lines of the ink design. The whole object is then covered with a thin layer of flux which when fired at a low temperature, fuses the wires to the body. Next, coloured enamel pastes are applied into the *cloisons*, the wires of which sit proud of the body surface. After the removal of any surplus paste, the object is ready for its first firing, usually at a temperature of between 800° and 900°C.

During firing the paste melts and contracts so in order to achieve a finished enamel of the same depth as the wires, the process of applying enamel paste and firing has to be repeated several times. To counter the effects of heat stress, counter-enamel is generally applied to the inside of the object. After each firing, any surplus hardened enamel is removed and the marks left by this process, together with any pit-marks or air-bubbles that have formed, are ground down before the next layer of enamel is applied. Finally, after all the *cloisons* have been filled with fired enamels to the required depth, the surface of the vessel is ground until the edges of the wires are visible, and then the whole piece is polished; this final process can in some instances take several months to complete. The craftsman may then gild the visible edges of the wires to create a more refined finish. Some vessels do not survive repeated firings and the success rate can sometimes be quite low.

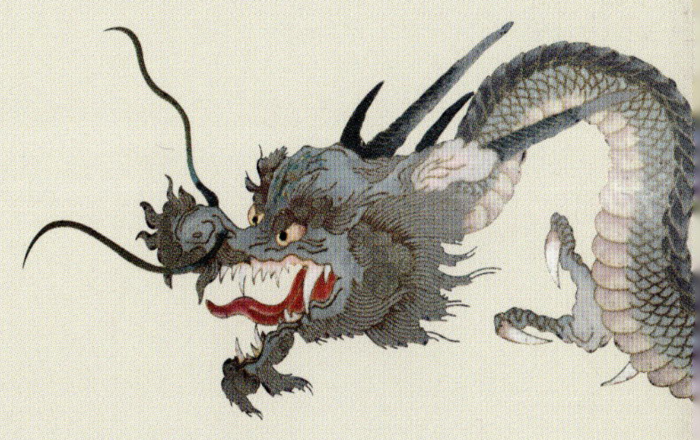

1
Group of six vases
showing some of the
basic processes of
cloisonné manufacture.

Unsigned, 1880–90.

Height (each vase) 8.9cm.

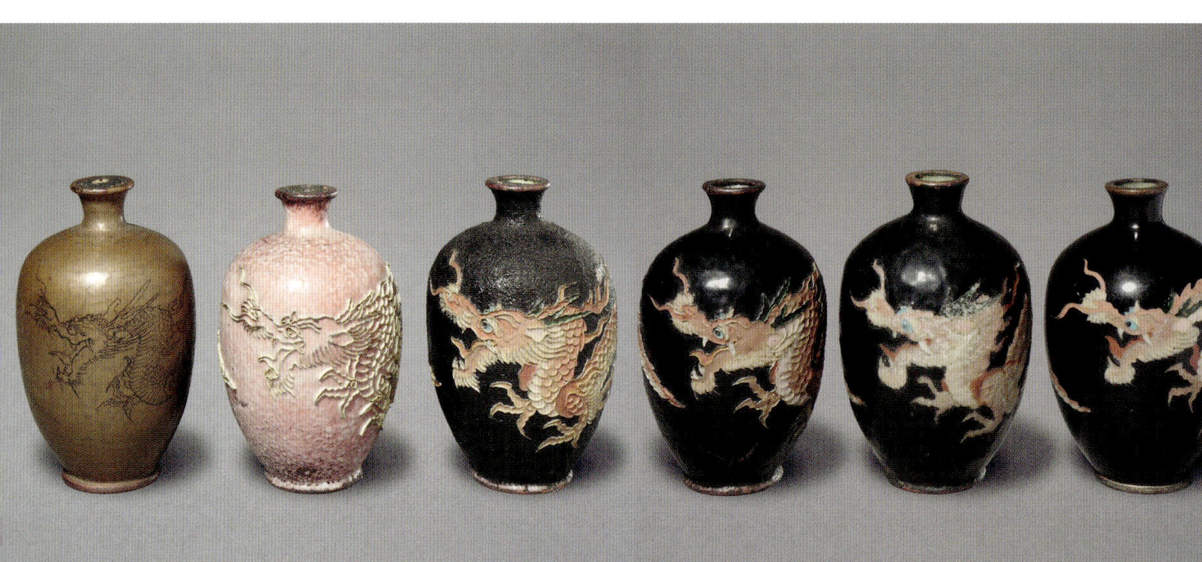

Vase (one of a pair) with decoration of a dragon; the lid is decorated with two *ho-o* birds and the gilded knob is in the form of a chrysanthemum.

Unsigned, Nagoya, *c.*1880–1900.

Height 24.9cm, diameter 24.9cm.

Henry Luis Florence Bequest

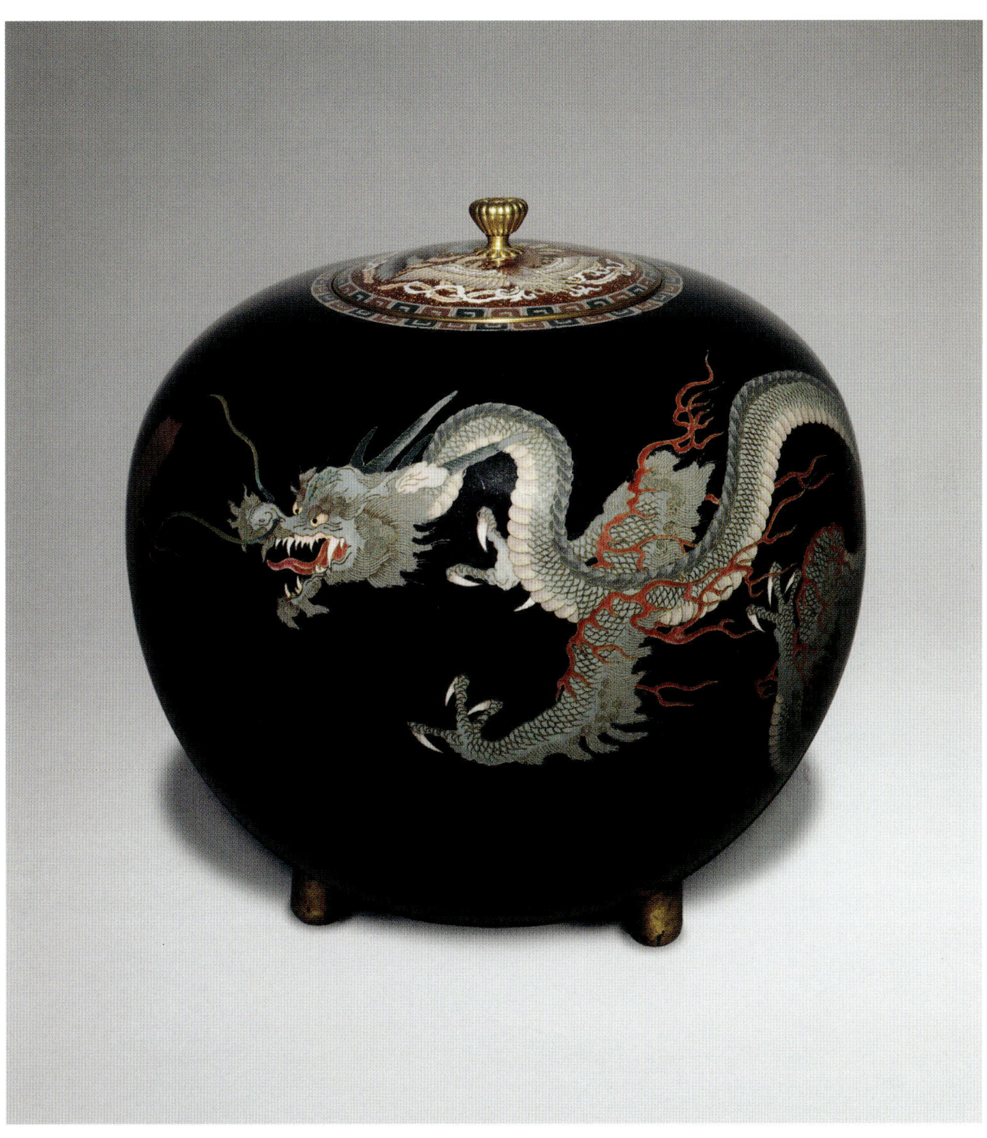

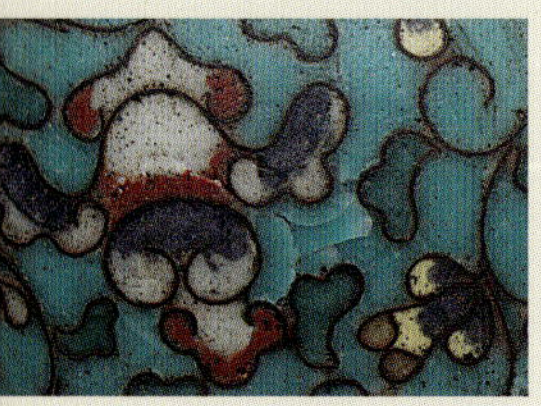

EARLY ENAMELS

One of the earliest examples of enamelwork in Japan is on a mirror in the Shosoin, the repository of imperial treasures in Nara. There has been much discussion over the date and provenance of this object: China, Korea and Japan have all been suggested as places of manufacture with dates ranging from the eighth to the early seventeenth century. There are few early examples of distinctly Japanese enamelling except for some small door fittings with enamelled designs in the Phoenix Hall (dedicated in 1053) of the Byodoin Temple, south of Kyoto, and cloisonné enamel-decorated architectural fittings used by the *shogun* Ashikaga Yoshimasa (1436–90) in his Higashiyama retreat in eastern Kyoto (now the Ginkakuji Temple).

In the late sixteenth century enamels became more widely used; as in earlier times, they were employed on architectural fittings, for example door-pulls (*hikite*; pl.3) and decorative nail covers (*kugi-kakushi*; pl.4). Many of these early enamels were not cloisonné in that they used few, if any, wires, but were executed mostly in the *champlevé* technique. True cloisonné enamelling was, however, used for the decoration of objects such as water-droppers (*suiteki*), which were part of writing sets and used in the preparation of ink (pl.5).

The most significant application of true cloisonné enamelling in pre-modern Japan was in the production of metal fittings for arms and armour. Under the patronage of the ruling military class, metalworkers of the late sixteenth century produced fine enamel decoration on the fittings associated with the mounted sword. The finest of these were made by the Hirata school, founded by Hirata Donin (died 1646), which was active through a subsequent eleven generations, well into the second half of the nineteenth century.

The Hirata school made small enamelled components, generally using gold wires to create the design and often employing a gold background to enhance the reflective qualities of the enamels; these were then applied or inlaid into sword fittings (pl.6). While the quality of the work of the Hirata school was generally very high, by the nineteenth century the term 'Hirata' was also used to refer to much less refined work in the style of the school but made by other craftsmen. Writing in 1895, James L. Bowes mentions that '… In more recent days, members of the family [Hirata] have been employed by the Imperial government as medallists' (Bowes 1895, p.81).

Although Chinese enamelled vessels had been imported and highly valued since at least the seventeenth century, there was, at least according to tradition, apparently no production of three-dimensional cloisonné-enamel objects in Japan until well into the nineteenth century. There are, however, a few larger-scale cloisonné objects that could have been made in Japan at an earlier date. On both technical and stylistic grounds, the ewer in pl.7 would normally be dated to around 1860, but an identical object in the Kyoto National Museum has been dated by some Japanese authorities to the late eighteenth or early nineteenth century (Suzuki, p.91). Japanese craftsmen had, for centuries, been able to adapt their skills to imported technology, so it is questionable whether they were not able to reproduce cloisonné enamels in the round.

3

Door-pull (*hikite*) of four-
lobed shape (*mokkogata*)
decorated in *champlevé*
(*zogan*) enamels.

Unsigned, *c*.1700.

Length 9.1cm, width 8cm.

4

Decorative nail-cover
(*kugi-kakushi*) decorated
in cloisonné and *champlevé*
enamels with a russet iron
plaque showing a bird
in flight.

Unsigned, *c*.1750–1800.

Height 6.2cm, width 8.8cm.

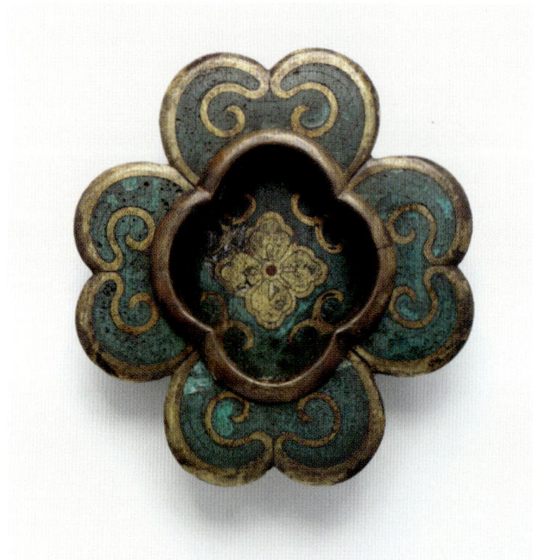

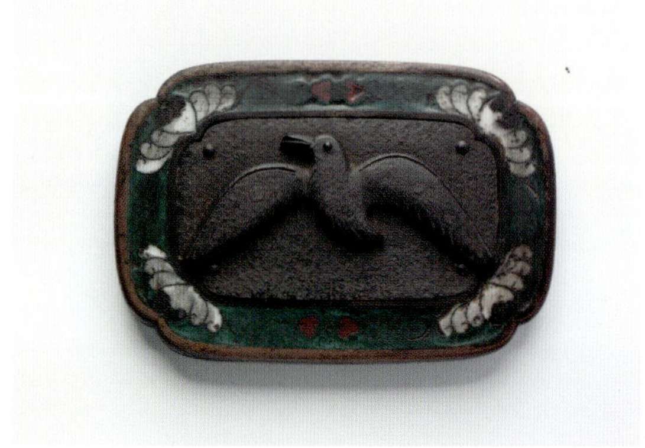

5
Water-dropper (*suiteki*)
decorated with cloud
motifs and stylized
floral scrolls.

Unsigned, *c.*1700–1800.

Height 4.1cm,
length 8.7cm.

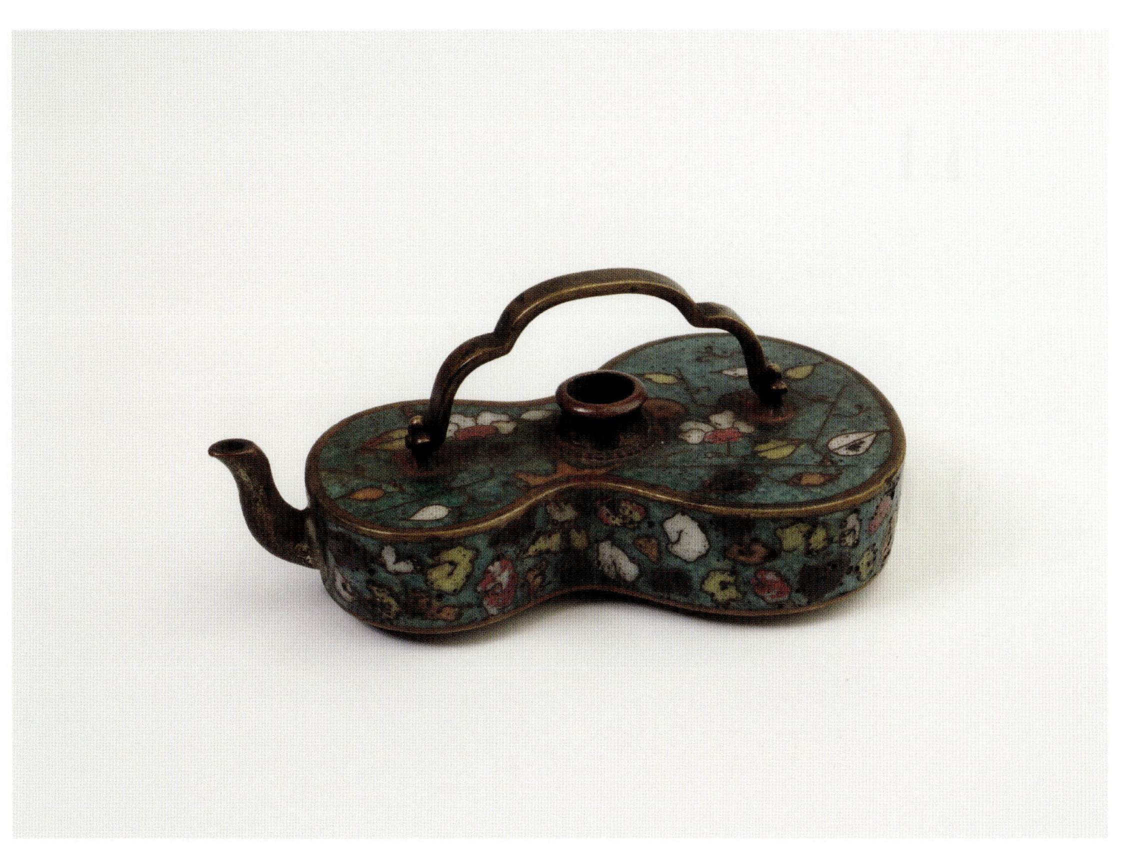

6

Pommel and collar (*fuchi-kashira*) from a sword hilt with applied gold-wire *cloisonné* enamel decoration of floral motifs, pine needles and spirals on a *shakudo* ground.

Unsigned, Hirata school *c.*1700–1800.

Length (*fuchi*) 3.7cm, length (*kashira*) 3.4cm.

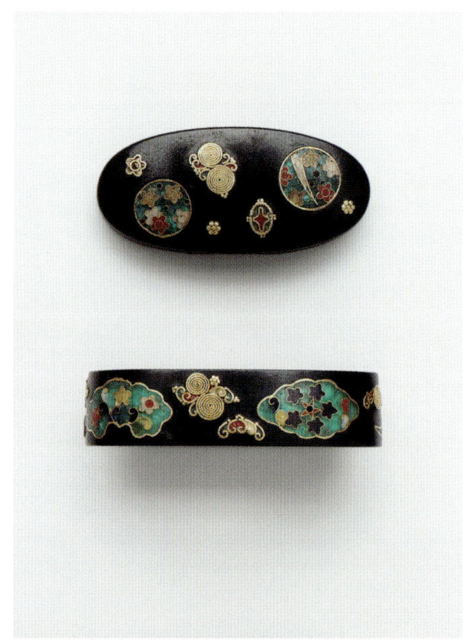

7

Hot-water ewer (*yuto*)
with decoration of
mythical creatures,
including dragons,
ho-o birds and *kirin*.

Unsigned, *c.* 1780–1840.

Height 18.3cm.

Bought from the
collection of Frederick,
Lord Leighton

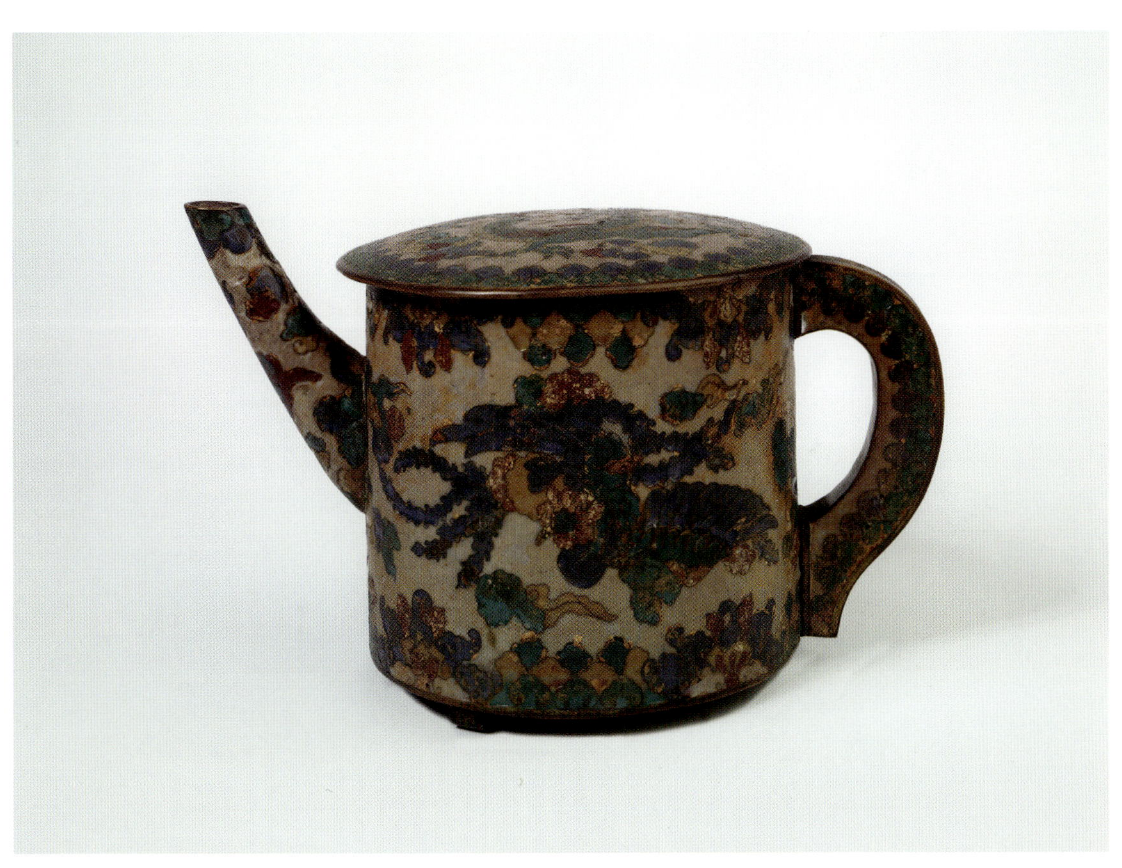

8

Inro, *ojime* (bead)
and netsuke (toggle)
decorated with lotus
flowers and scrolls on
a *shinchu* ground. An
inro is a traditional
Japanese case for
holding small objects
such as personal seals
or medicines.

Unsigned, *c.* 1800–50.

Length 6.35cm,
width 5.72cm.

9

Possibly a water-dropper
(*suiteki*) decorated
with abstract motifs.
A similar piece,
illustrated in Coben and
Ferster, pl.14, is fitted as
a pricket candlestick.

Unsigned, *c.* 1750–1800.

Height 6.86cm.

Gift of Lady Orchardson

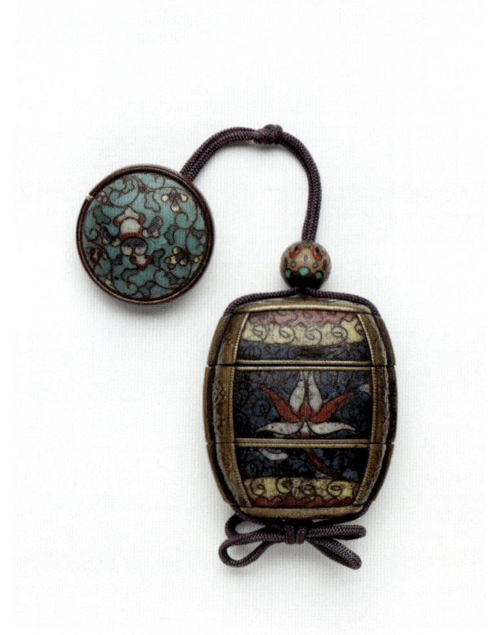

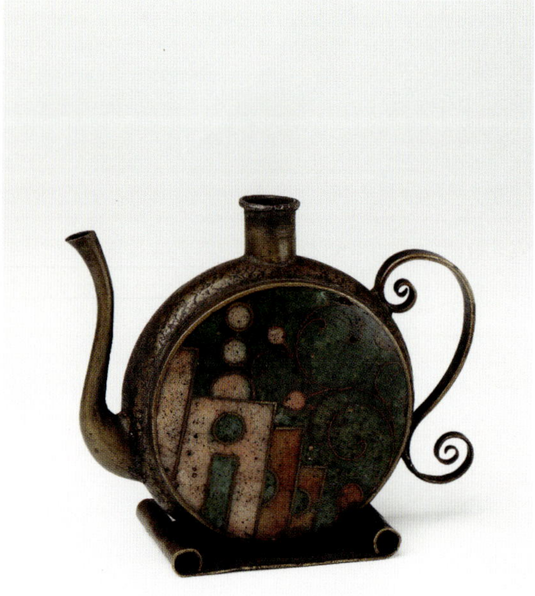

Cast-iron sake kettle (*choshi*) with decoration of pine and abstract motifs; the handle is inlaid with silver chrysanthemums and *shippo* motifs and the cloisonné-enamel lid has an ivory knob on a *shippo* roundel.

Unsigned, *c.*1750–1800.

Height 15.3cm, width 19.8cm.

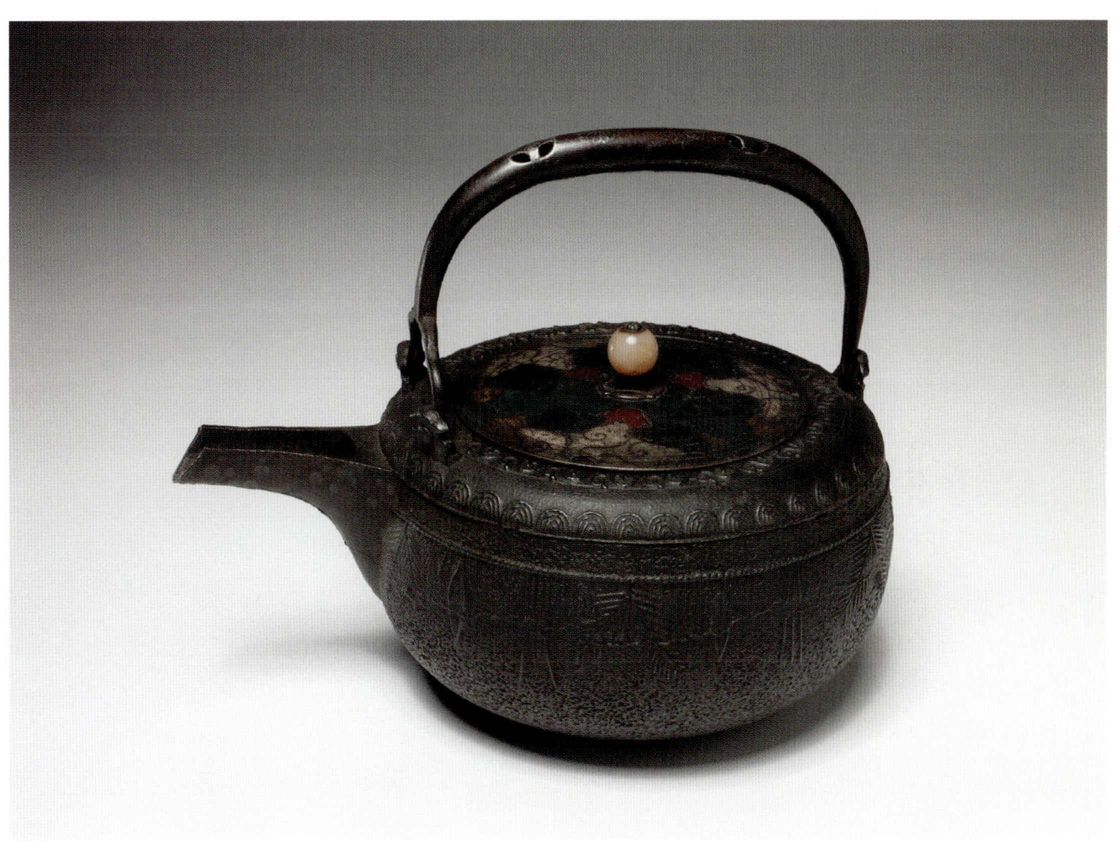

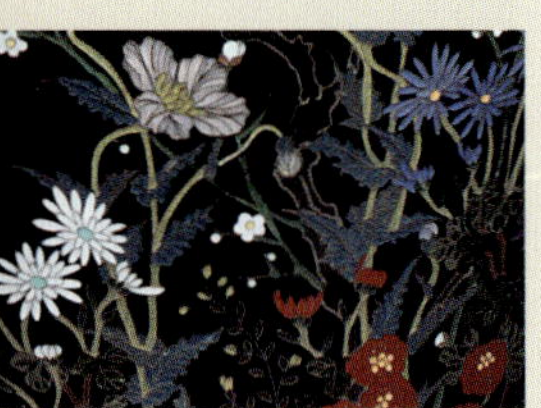

THE RENAISSANCE OF JAPANESE CLOISONNÉ

One thing, however, is certain; namely that until the nineteenth century enamels were employed by the Japanese decorators for accessory purposes only. No such things were manufactured as vases, plaques, censers or bowls having their surface covered with enamels applied either in the champlevé or the cloisonné style… prior to the year 1838.
(Brinkley, Vol.VII, pp.330–31)

The renaissance of Japanese cloisonné manufacture is credited to Kaji Tsunekichi (1803–83) of Nagoya in Owari province (modern Aichi prefecture), a former samurai turned metal-gilder. Like many other samurai of the early nineteenth century he was forced to find ways to supplement his meagre official stipend. The generally accepted story is that around 1838 Kaji acquired a piece of Chinese (or by some unlikelier accounts, Dutch) cloisonné enamel and, by taking it apart and examining how it was made, managed to produce a small cloisonné-enamel dish. Then, according to Brinkley's summary of Kaji's own account of his career, 'He now applied himself with patient assiduity to work of this kind, and succeeded, in 1839, in making a plate six inches in diameter' (Brinkley, Vol.VII, p.334). Kaji then produced other small items, such as brush-rests and cups, and soon 'had the honour of seeing his productions presented to the Tokugawa Court in Yedo by the feudal chief (*daimyo*) of Owari' (Brinkley, Vol.VII, p.334). By the late 1850s Kaji had been appointed official cloisonné maker to the *daimyo* of Owari.

Basing his designs on the motifs and colour schemes of Chinese cloisonné enamels, Kaji drew upon the resources and expertise of other metalworkers and potters (who had the skills required to fire his enamel pieces) to realize his ambitions. He had many technical difficulties to overcome and his early works, like those of other makers of the time, are characterized by the use of a larger number of background wires for both decorative and practical reasons. The patterns created by the wires on these early pieces often took the form of stylized waves, clouds, key-fret patterns and scrolling *karakusa* (Chinese grasses). The few extant works that can definitely be attributed to Kaji include a temple bowl in the Shomyoji Temple (pl.12 in Coben and Ferster and similar to the bowl in pl.15). This was later exhibited by the Nagoya Cloisonné Company (Nagoya Shippo Kaisha) in the Second Industrial Exposition of 1881 though with no mention of the name of Kaji (Meiji no Takara, p.22).

By the mid 1850s Kaji was sufficiently confident to start taking on pupils, including Hayashi Shogoro (d.1896), a craftsman mainly celebrated for the fact that his own pupils were teachers of many of the later masters of cloisonné enamelling. The most significant of Hayashi's pupils was Tsukamoto Kaisuke (1828–87), who studied under him from 1860–61. Kaisuke is believed to have been responsible for the discovery, some time around 1868, of how to apply cloisonné enamels to a ceramic vessel (pl.17). Brinkley noted, 'Since 1868 the Owari [Nagoya] potters have introduced an entirely novel method of decorating porcelain, by cloisonné enamelling' (Brinkley, Vol. VIII, p.297).

Tsukamoto Kaisuke in turn taught Hayashi Kodenji (1831–1915), a craftsman who was to become one of the most influential cloisonné makers of his time. Hayashi set up an independent cloisonné workshop in Nagoya in 1862 and, like his teacher, began to train other craftsmen. He remained at the forefront of cloisonné manufacturing in the Nagoya region throughout his career (pl.19). In 1871 the Nagoya Cloisonné Company was established at Toshima, just outside Nagoya, by Muramatsu Hikoshichi and Tsukamoto Jine'mon, the elder brother of Tsukamoto Kaisuke. The technological advances they made resulted in the company winning a first prize at the Vienna Exhibition of 1873 (Harris, p.111). Many cloisonné-manufacturing companies sprang up in and around Toshima and the area rapidly became Japan's main centre of cloisonné production. It has been estimated that at their peak the cloisonné manufactories of Toshima were producing 'no less than seventy percent of the total cloisonné enamels produced in Japan' (Harada, p.278).

From tentative beginnings in Nagoya in the 1830s, there had been a rapid increase in the production of cloisonné enamels in the 1850s and the ensuing obsession in the West for all forms of Japanese art ensured a ready market. Following the downfall of the samurai government and the restoration to power of the emperor in 1868, Japanese artisans, especially metalworkers, lost their traditional patrons and had to find new markets for their skills. As Japan strove to throw off its feudal past and develop as a modern industrialized and economic power, so the West, which had until then seen very little Japanese art except lacquerware and porcelain made for export, suddenly developed a voracious appetite for the artistic products of the country. Adopting the slogan *Wakon Yosai* (Japanese spirit, western knowledge), Japan employed western technicians and advisers to work with Japanese craftsmen on the introduction of new and improved methods of production. This was also the time when great exhibitions were being held all over the world and at these occasions Japan displayed its skills in arts, crafts and other manufacturing industries. The production of cloisonné enamels had, by the end of the nineteenth century, expanded to become one of Japan's most successful forms of manufacture and export.

Sir Rutherford Alcock, one of Britain's first diplomats in Japan and organizer of the Japanese display at the 1862 London International Exhibition commented on cloisonné enamels:

> Their patterns are generally intricate and minute, small sprays, flowers, diapers, and geometrical figures all being laid under contribution, while leaves of various colours – drab, white, light green – are interspersed. These being minutely subdivided, it is impossible not to be struck with admiration at the marvellous delicacy of execution and fertility of invention, if not of imagination, displayed. Such works would simply be unproducible in any country where skilled workmanship of a high order, and artistic in kind, was not abundant and obtainable at exceedingly low rates of remuneration. Many of the enamel works must represent the labour of years, even for two or three hands. (Alcock, p.190)

Another commentator was James Lord Bowes who had acquired a large collection of Japanese art, including numerous pieces of cloisonné enamels, and was among the earliest of collectors in the West to write in detail on the subject. He had extremely adamant views about the history and development of Japanese cloisonné, many of which were simply wrong. He classified Japanese enamels into groups which, under his scheme, placed many objects in the eighteenth or even seventeenth centuries. His views were criticized by many of his contemporaries for being totally out of keeping with what was known at the time yet many of his theories persisted until the late twentieth century.

In 1901 Brinkley wrote:

> Mr Bowes maintained his views with remarkable firmness. No Japanese collection, public or private, contained any specimen of the wares which he supposed to have been produced and preserved in temples and noblemen's residences during nearly three centuries. No Japanese connoisseur had any knowledge of such objects having been manufactured previously to 1837… Some of the specimens which Mr Bowes attributed to the seventeenth century were unhesitatingly identified by artisans of the present time as their own work, and the signatures which certain of the specimens bore were claimed by the men who had actually signed them… he clung to that theory with a tenacity which, considering the testimony on the other side, is probably unique. (Brinkley, Vol.VII, pp.375–6)

It was possibly due to the experimental nature of Japanese cloisonné during these early years, and the fact that the vessels being made were often imitations of Chinese originals of earlier periods, that there was a supposition by many westerners – as with Bowes – that what they were looking at was ancient, when in fact the objects were frequently more or less contemporary. Charlotte M. Salwey explained in her 1906 presentation to the Japan Society:

> Today in some manufactories you may find specimens that bear all the appearance of great antiquity, with all the subtle cunning and workmanship of earlier archaic energy, but should you inquire of the master of the factory if he could furnish you with an approximate date of manufacture, he will smile a pleasing smile as he courteously makes answer 'These honourable pieces that you inquire about have just been withdrawn from the kiln today.'

11

Bowl decorated
with stylized flowers
(including lotus or
hosoge), fine *karakusa*
and dish decorated
with two dragons on a
ground of clouds and
karakusa scrolls.

Unsigned, Nagoya,
1850–60.

Diameter (dish) 20.9cm;
height (bowl) 8.3cm,
diameter 17.2 cm.

Bequest of Eleanor Watt

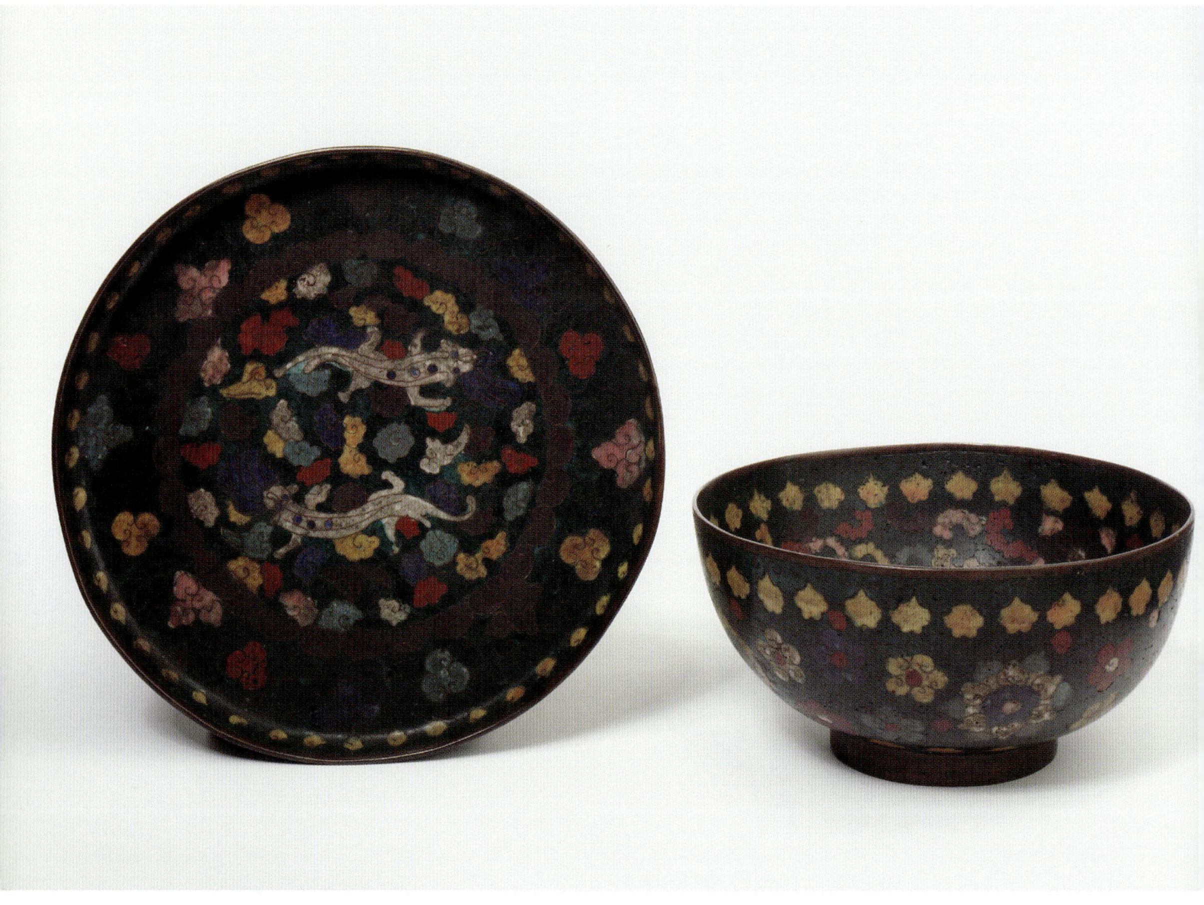

Stem cup decorated
with floral motifs and
a carp inside the bowl.

Signed 'Bushu
Takayama kore o
tsukuru' (Made by
[or at] Takayama
in Bushu [Musashi]
province), *c.*1800–50.

Height 11.8cm,
diameter 7.2cm.

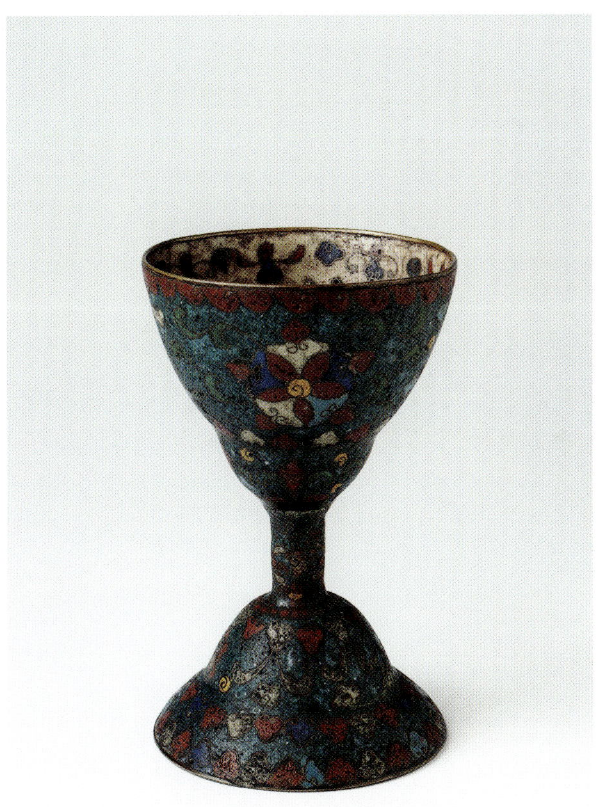

13

Dish decorated with a
central panel of three
sprites (*shojo*) and a
large sake flask; the
borders have abstract
floral motifs and
fan-shaped panels
containing various
birds. At the time
of acquisition the
V&A records state,
'an undoubted piece
by the founder of
Japanese Cloisonné
Enamels in large
objects, Kaji
Tsunekichi… .'

Unsigned, Nagoya,
c. 1850–60.

Diameter 73.7cm.

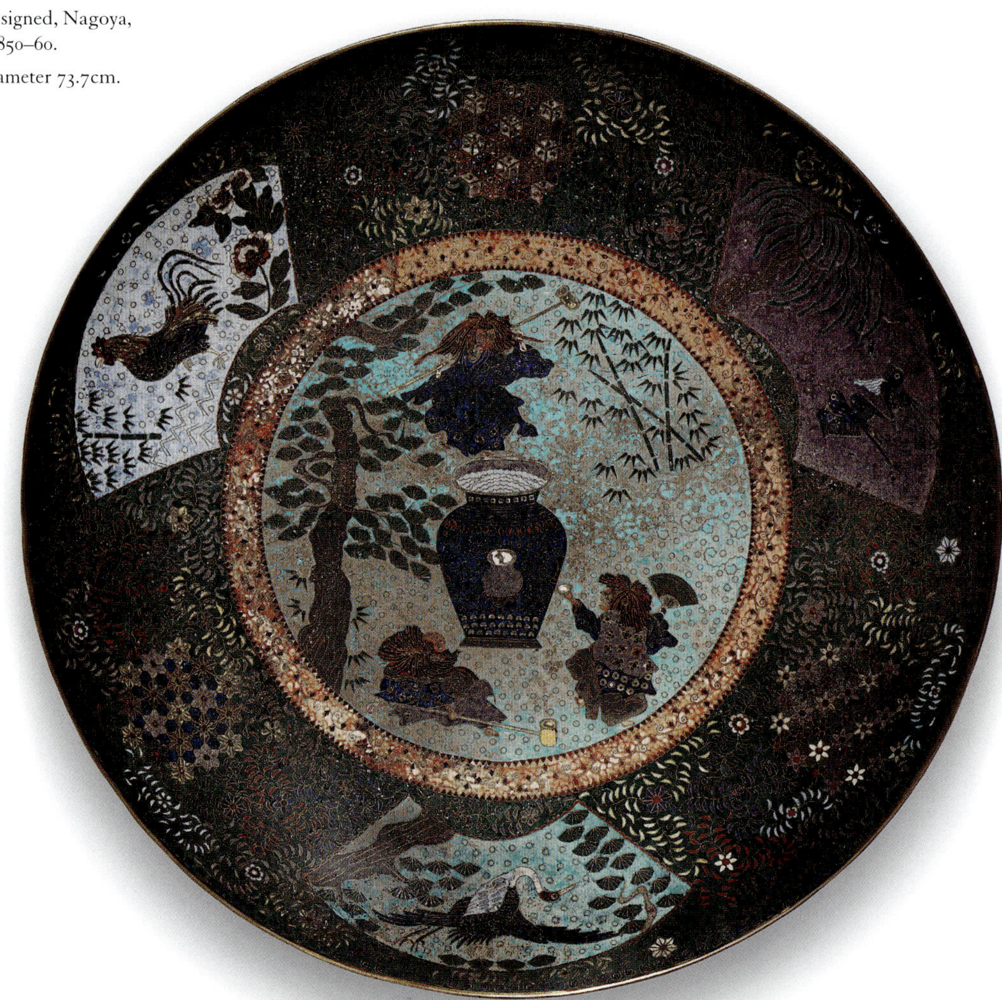

14

Covered bowl with
decoration of panels
containing sea shells
and seaweed on a
ground decorated
with peonies, *karakusa*
and floral scrolls.

Unsigned, Nagoya,
*c.*1860–75.

Height 20.9cm,
diameter 23.2cm.

15

Water-container
(*mizusashi*) decorated
with a mythical beast,
stylized lotus or *hosoge*
flowers and geometric
motifs. The base carries
the Japanese character
raku (pleasure) in red
enamel. The bowl is
similar in many respects
to a documented
temple bowl by Kaji
Tsunekichi.

Unsigned, Nagoya,
*c.*1860–70.

Height 9.9cm,
diameter 14.1cm.

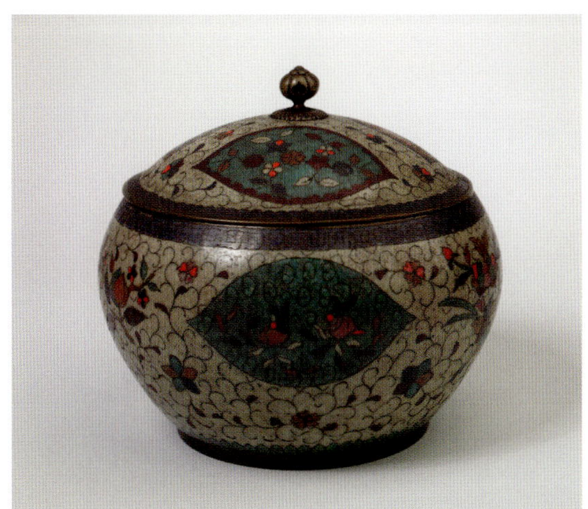

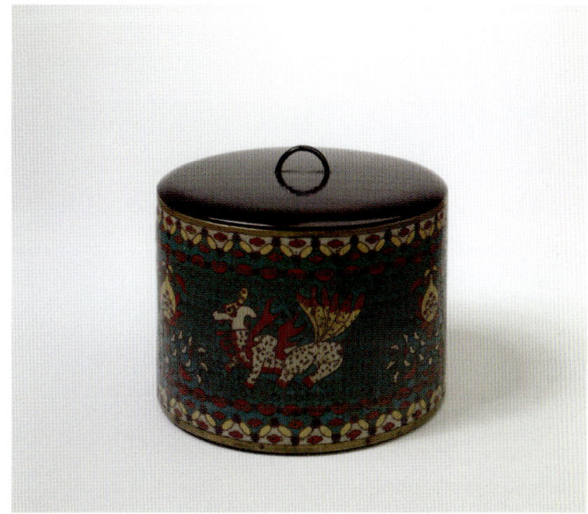

16

Vase decorated with floral and abstract patterns and a panel containing a carp leaping through a waterfall.

Unsigned, Nagoya, *c.*1865–75.

Height 63.5cm.

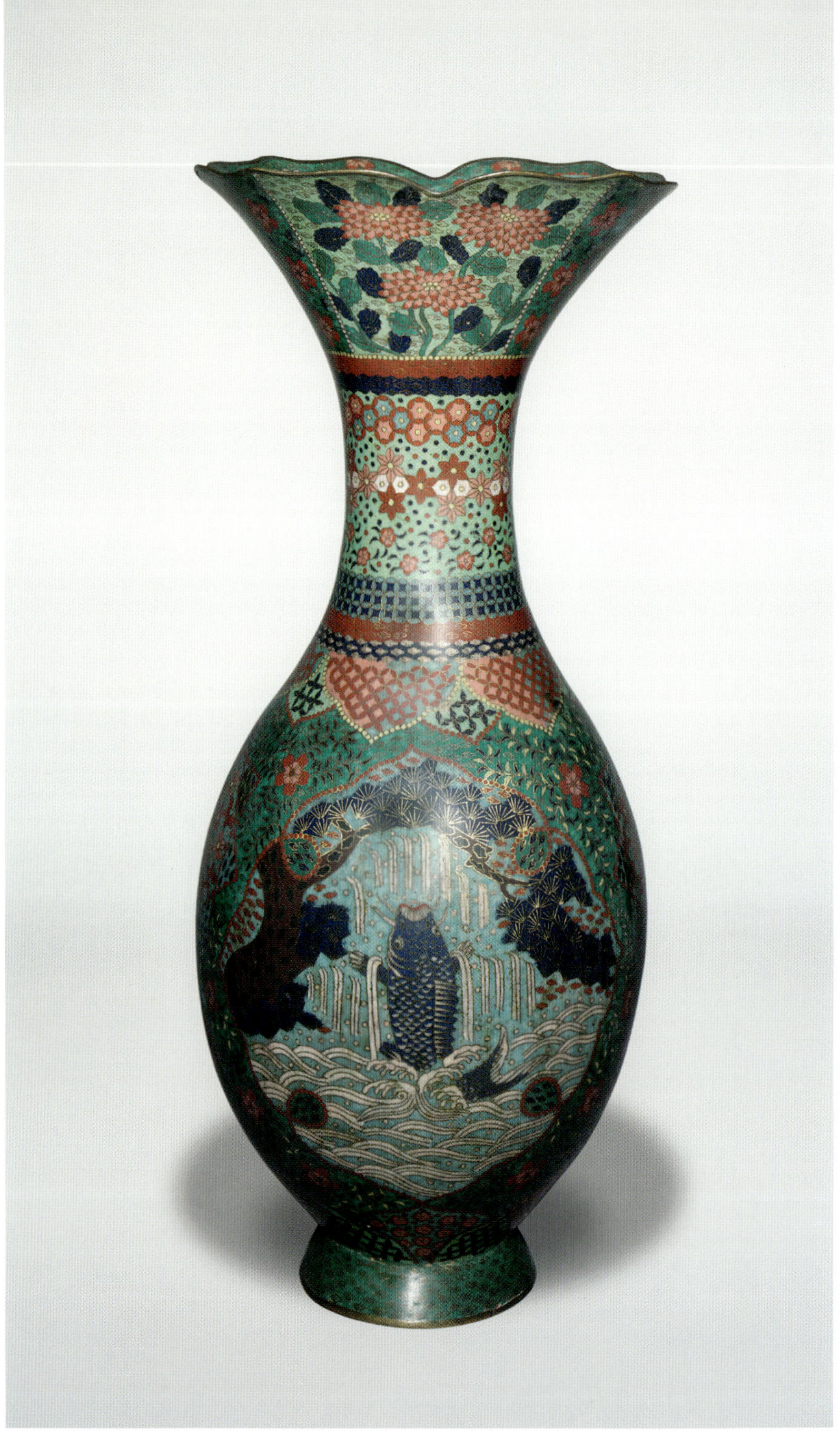

17

Porcelain bowl in
underglaze blue, the
exterior decorated
with abstract and
floral cloisonné
enamels.

Unsigned, Nagoya,
*c.*1870–75.

Height 9.53cm,
diameter 17.15cm.

18

Lidded porcelain tea
container (*natsume*).

Signed 'Dai Nihon
Aichi ken Hara Fujio
zo' (Made by Hara Fuji
of Aichi prefecture in
Great Japan), Nagoya,
*c.*1870–80.

Height (with lid)
10.2cm.

Gift of Sir Harry Garner

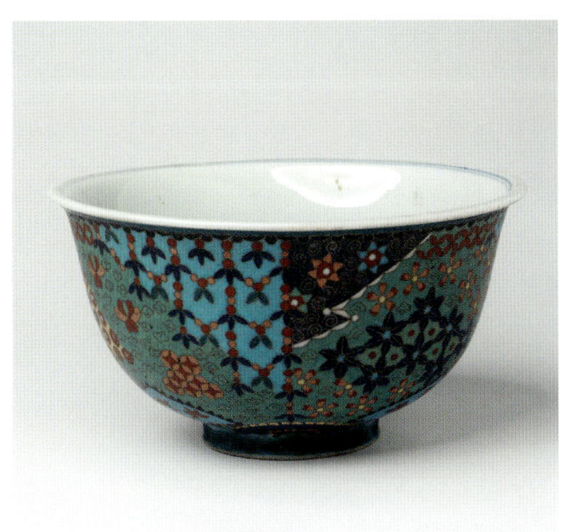

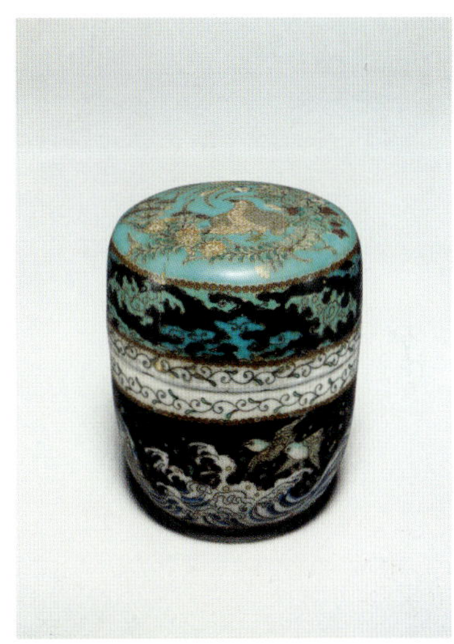

19

Vase with dark blue-
black enamel ground
and silver-wire design of
butterflies, the curves in
their bodies defined with
the use of fine wires.

Signed 'Aichi Hayashi
Kodenji', Nagoya,
*c.*1880–90.

Height 25cm, width 12cm.

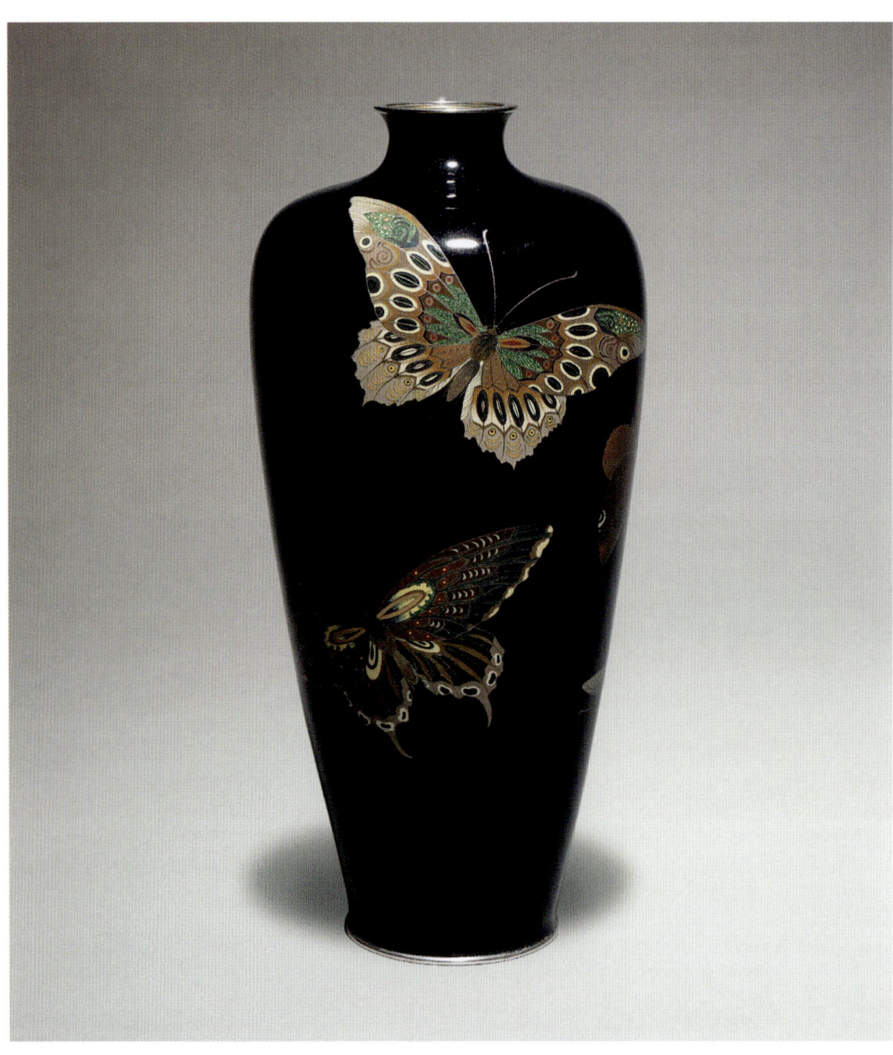

20

Vase with *nanako* ground
and a design of carp in
weed, enamelled in the
akasuke technique.

Signed 'Nagoya Hayashi
Ko[denji]' and with mark
of Hayashi Kodenji,
Nagoya, *c.*1890.

Height 9.5cm, width 6.5cm.

21

Vase with silver rims
and silver-wire
decoration of
chrysanthemums and
other flowers with a
bird perched on a branch
of plum blossom.

Mark of Hayashi
Kodenji, Nagoya,
*c.*1880–85.

Height 15cm, width 7cm.

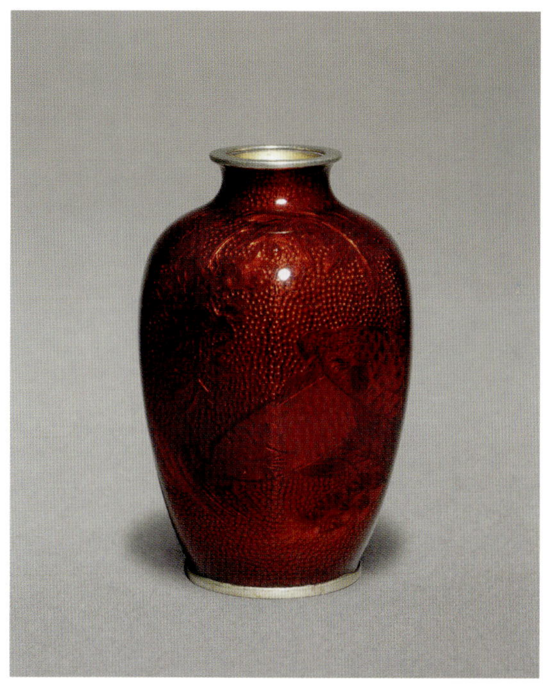

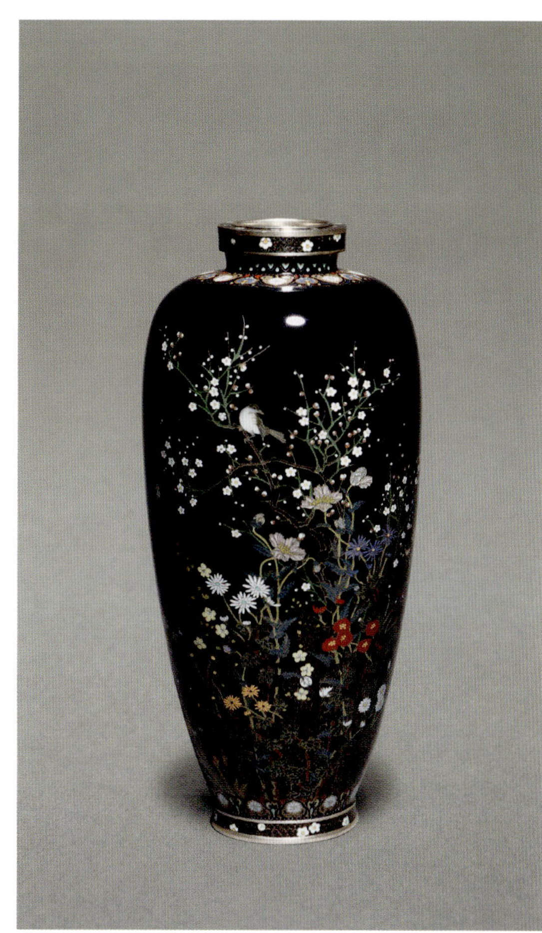

22

Vase with pale grey
enamel ground
decorated with a design
of exotic butterflies,
their bodies delineated
with silver wire of
varied thickness.

Signed 'Aichi Hayashi
Ko[denji]', Nagoya,
*c.*1880–90.

Height 12.5cm,
width 7.5cm.

23

Vase with silver-wire
decoration of two exotic
long-tailed birds in
bamboo and flowering
shrubs on a rich blue
enamel ground typically
associated with Nagoya
makers.

Unsigned, possibly
Hayashi Kodenji,
Nagoya, *c.*1895–1900.

Height 31.5cm,
width 19cm.

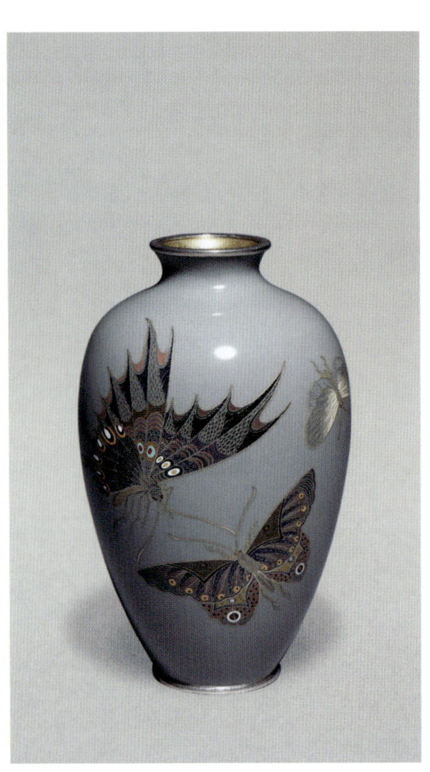

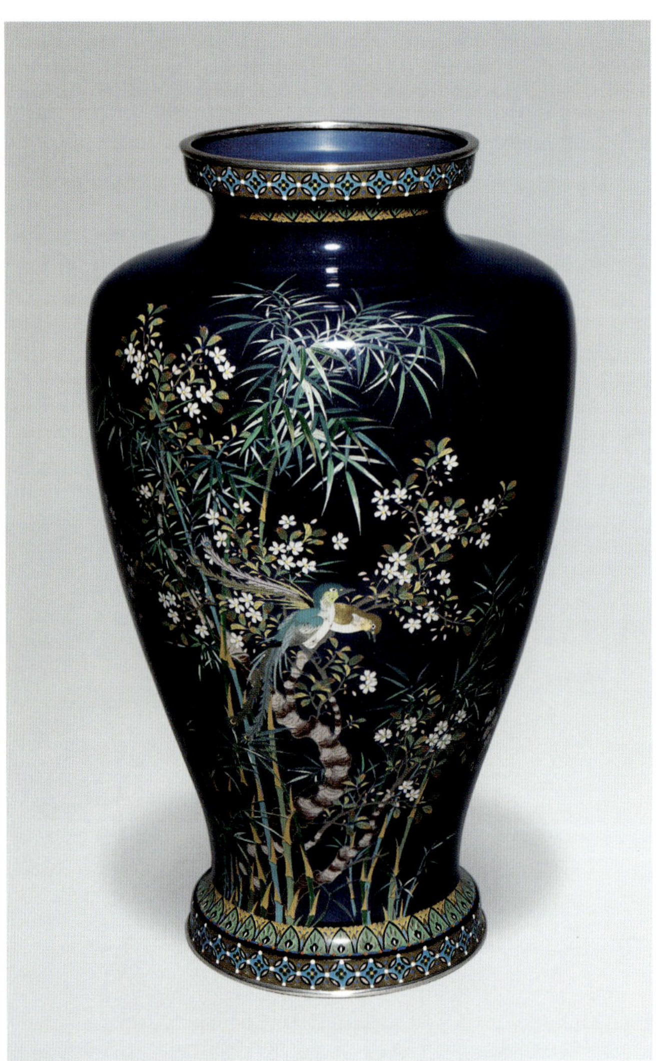

24

Pair of vases each with
a design of purple and
white irises beside rocks
and a swirling stream,
one vase representing
daytime, the other night.

Signed 'Dai Nihon Aichi
Hayashi Saku' (Made
by Hayashi [Kodenji]
of Aichi prefecture, Great
Japan), Nagoya, *c.* 1910.

Height 24.5cm,
width 13cm.

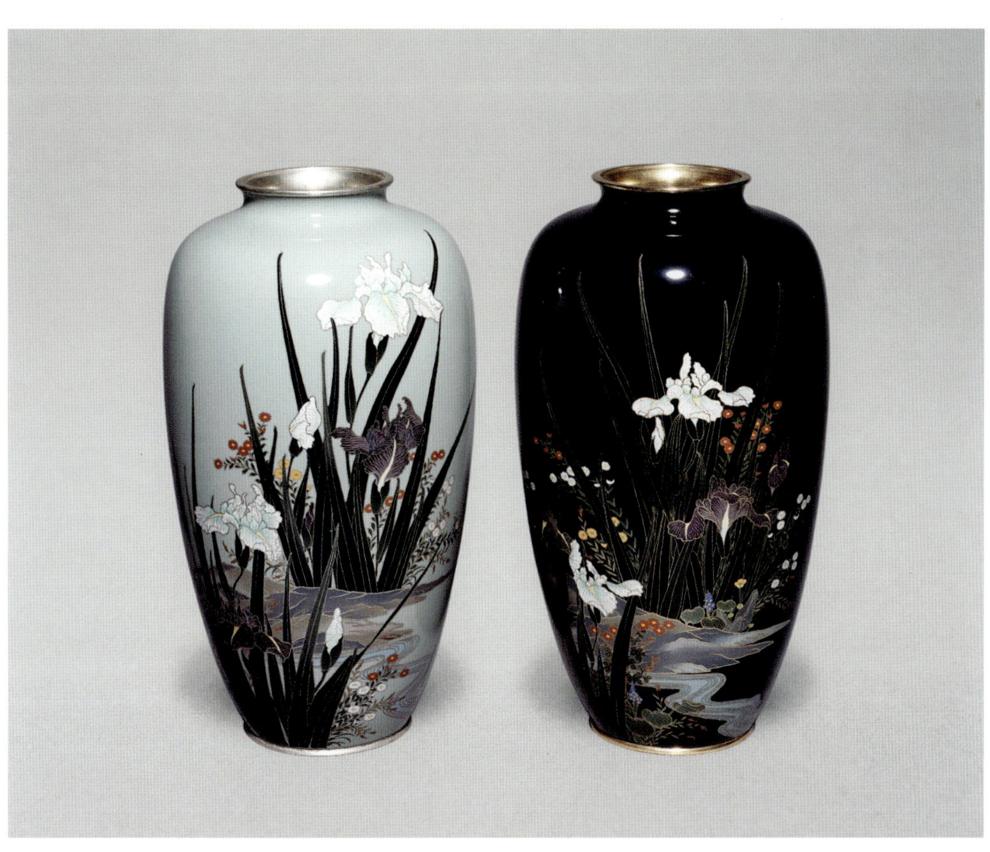

25

Ewer or teapot decorated with pine trees, a *ho-o* bird and floral motifs.

Unsigned, Nagoya, *c.*1880–90.

Height (with handle) 15.24cm, diameter 14.61cm.

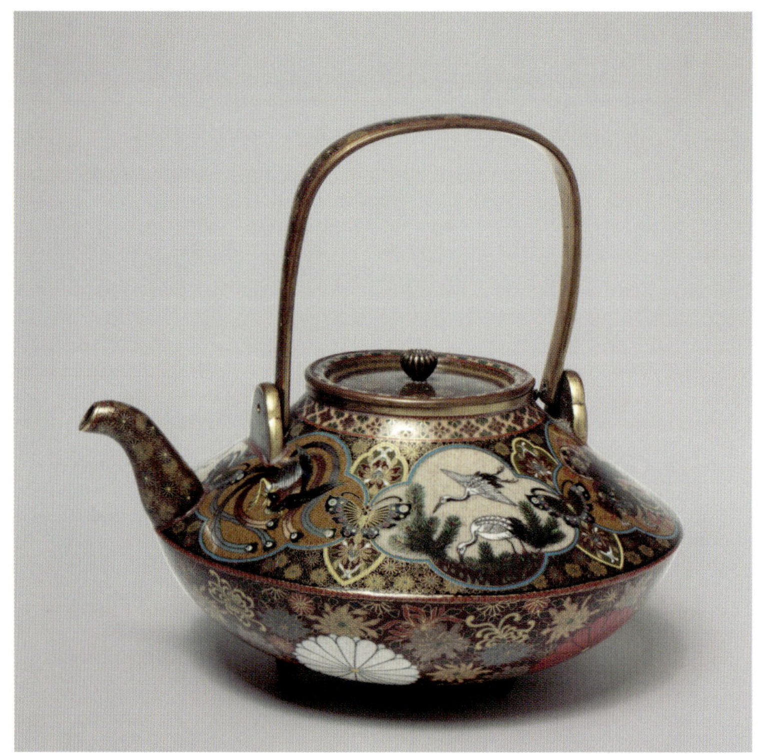

26

Lidded vessel decorated with a central panel of two dragons; above and below are foliate panels containing mythical creatures including *ho-o* birds and the *shachi*, a mythical sea creature commonly associated with Nagoya.

Unsigned, but attributed at the time of acquisition to 'Namikawa of Kyoto' but later to Honda Yosaburo, Nagoya, *c.*1880–1890.

Height 21.59cm, width 24.13cm.

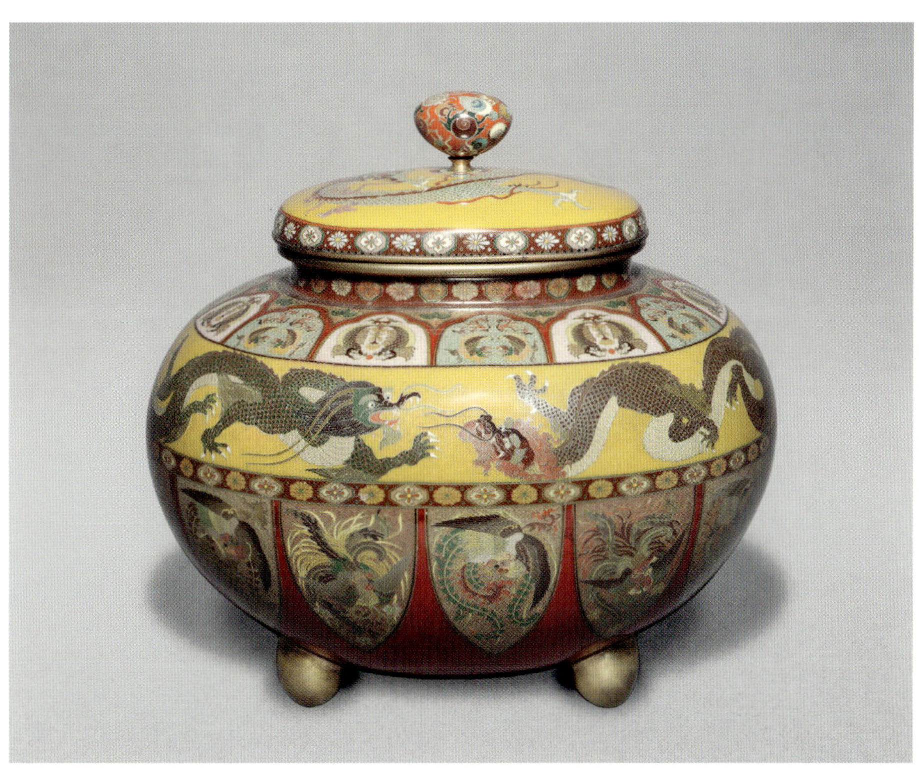

THE GOLDEN AGE

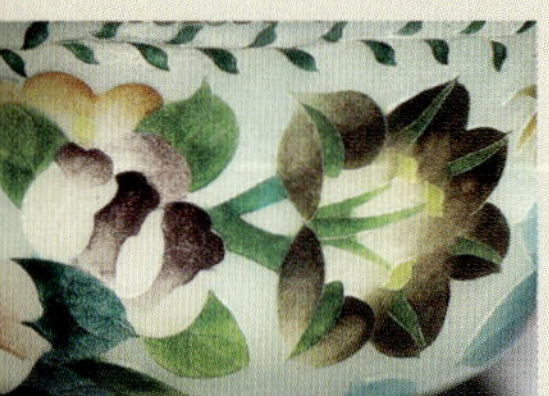

The peak of artistic and technological sophistication lasted from around 1880 to 1910, a period often referred to as the 'Golden Age' of Japanese enamels. During this time there were hundreds of workshops of varying sizes and degrees of ability working to satisfy the demand of what was predominantly a western export market.

By 1875, Tsukamoto Kaisuke had left Nagoya to become the chief foreman of the Ahrens Company in Tokyo. Ahrens was one of many companies set up under the new Meiji government's programme wherein western specialists were invited to help modernize Japan's existing industries. The chief technologist of Ahrens was the German chemist Gottfried Wagener (1831–92), an expert on glazes and firing techniques, who introduced modern European enamelling technology to Japan. He and Tsukamoto were responsible for many of the key innovations on which the Japanese cloisonné-enamel industry was to depend. Their collaboration created enamels with a wider range, depth and intensity of colours; finishes were improved and far higher levels of gloss were now achievable. Other innovations introduced by Wagener eliminated much of the need for background wires to retain the enamels, and thus the application of clear bright enamels over large unbroken areas of a vessel's surface could be achieved. No longer were patterns of circles, abstract patterns and *karakusa* scrolls required for purely technical reasons and the creation of more realistic and painterly enamel designs was now possible.

In 1878 the Ahrens Company closed down and Wagener moved to Kyoto; Tsukamoto returned to Nagoya where he found employment with the Nagoya Cloisonné Company. In Kyoto, Wagener met the former samurai, now cloisonné artist, Namikawa Yasuyuki (1845–1927). Yasuyuki began his artistic career around 1868 and worked with the Kyoto Cloisonné Company (Kyoto Shippo Kaisha) from 1871 to 1874. Having then established his own studio, he began to exhibit his work at national and international exhibitions including Philadelphia, 1876,

the First National Industrial Exhibition, Tokyo, 1877 and
Paris, 1878 (Meiji no Takara, p.30; pl.27). Although it is not
clear how Wagener and Yasuyuki met, there is no doubt that
they collaborated and that the most significant end result was
the creation of the superb semi-transparent mirror-black
enamel that was to become the hallmark of much of Yasuyuki's
subsequent work (pl.28).

Yasuyuki's enamel wares are characterized by the skilful
use of intricate wirework and the superb attention to detail.
The designs on his earlier pieces consisted mainly of stylized
botanical and formal geometric motifs, while his later work
tended to be more pictorial with scenes from nature and views
of landmarks in and around Kyoto. His work included objects
with designs predominantly defined by wires as well as pieces
where the pictorial composition is balanced by large areas of
pure coloured enamel (pl.28). Yasuyuki strove to improve both
his technical and artistic skills and continued to exhibit his
cloisonné wares at the national industrial exhibitions. In 1896
he was appointed Imperial Craftsman (*Teishitsu Gigei'in*) to the
court of the Emperor Meiji. This was an important position
and guaranteed a domestic market for his work while simulta-
neously increasing its value and price. Yasuyuki retired in 1915
and his company closed soon afterwards.

It was to Yasuyuki's studio that many western travellers to
Japan ventured, often leaving extensive descriptions of what
they saw. By all accounts Yasuyuki was easier-going than other
producers and was more than happy to entertain the steady
stream of western visitors who called on him. One of the most
detailed descriptions of Yasuyuki and his workshop is to be
found in Herbert Ponting's *In Lotus Land Japan,* where an
entire chapter is devoted to the subject (Ponting, pp.53–67).
His studio, which survives today as the Namikawa Museum
– its garden largely unchanged since Ponting's time – was, and
still is, relaxing and serene. In Yasuyuki's workshop Ponting
observed:

> Each member of staff has absorbed the master's ideas
> from his earliest acquaintance with the art; and although
> Namikawa now does little work himself except designing
> and firing he closely supervises each piece during its entire
> execution... His artists do not work by set hours, but only
> when the mental inspiration is upon them... .
> (Ponting, pp.65–7; pl.30)

Namikawa Sosuke (1847–1910) was another important cloi-sonné artist who was also appointed Imperial Craftsman in 1896. Much to the confusion of contemporary western visitors to Japan, Sosuke and Yasuyuki were unrelated, the family name of Namikawa being written with different characters. Sosuke originally worked for the Nagoya Cloisonné Company but later moved to run the company branch in Tokyo. Coben and Ferster state that Sosuke did not build a factory in Tokyo until 1887, however, in an undated publicity brochure issued by Sosuke (which includes an interview with Sosuke in the *New York Herald* dated 9 February 1896), there is an extract from the reports of the judges of the Third National Exhibi-tion, Tokyo, 1890, which states that '... in April of the follow-ing year [1880] the [Nagoya Cloisonné] Company established a factory at Ushigome, Tokyo, and placed it under the manage-ment and superintendency of Mr S. Namikawa'.

Sosuke was an active contributor to both national and inter-national expositions winning prizes at the 1883 Amsterdam Universal Exposition, the 1885 Nuremberg International Met-alwork Exhibition and the 1889 Paris Exposition Universelle. He employed Jinsuke and Jinkuro, the sons of Tsukamoto Kaisuke and thanks to their technical expertise Sosuke per-fected a distinctive style of decoration in which his enamels appeared to reproduce ink paintings. The two techniques he used, *shosen* and *musen*, depended on enamels that would not bleed into each other when not separated by wires. In the case of *shosen* ('few', or 'limited' wires), the number of wires was kept to a minimum and they were used only to delineate small details, while in *musen* (literally 'no wires'), the wires were removed prior to the final firing. The term 'cloisonné', with regard to these developments, now became somewhat redun-dant as this style of enamelling no longer employed *cloisons*.

Sosuke reproduced historical paintings and worked closely with contemporary painters, notably Watanabe Seitei (1851–1918). At the World's Columbian Exhibition of 1893 he exhib-ited *Mount Fuji among the Clouds*, a large plaque in wireless shaded enamels; this subject was reworked by Sosuke in a number of versions and was copied by other manufacturers. It was at about this time that Sosuke, a man not shy to tell the world about his achievements, began to use the character '*saki-gake*' (meaning 'pioneer') as a seal on his work (pl.36).

Nagoya and the surrounding area continued to be the major centre of cloisonné manufacture where many makers established their workshops producing wares in different styles and in varying quality. However, none was more influential and productive than the Ando Company, founded by Ando Jubei in 1880. Its foreman from 1881 to 1897 was Kaji Sataro, grand son of Kaji Tsunekichi; he was succeeded by Kawade Shibataro (1856–1921?) who introduced and developed the numerous technical innovations on which the Ando Company's success was based (pl.41). His major development – sometimes credited to Hattori Tadasaburo, another Nagoya-based maker – was *moriage* (pl.42). This painstaking technique, which required extreme care, especially at the polishing stage, involved building up layers of enamel to produce a three-dimensional effect and was ideally suited to subjects such as plants and flowers.

Harada's description of the Ando Company mentions that as well as having 'one large factory', he 'also has many artists in different parts of Nagoya and Toshima working exclusively for him'. Kawade is given particular mention:

> [Ando's] reputation was established chiefly by the
> splendid work turned out by his chief enamel artist and
> designer, Kawade Shibataro, who is deservedly considered
> the greatest enamel expert in the manufacture of *shippo*
> at the present time. Perhaps no other living person
> has done more towards the improvement of Japanese
> enamels and the invention of new methods of application
> than Kawade.
> (Harada, pp.282–3)

The exact nature of the business relationship between Kawade and Ando is not clear. While there are vessels that carry Kawade's mark within the Ando mark, there are others that bear Kawade's mark alone and yet other pieces bearing the Ando mark that are clearly by Kawade (pl.43).

In the early 1900s the Ando Company began producing enamels in the technique called *plique-á-jour* (*shotai-jippo* in Japanese). Ando Jubei had seen examples at the Paris Exposition of 1900 and brought a piece by Fernand Thesmar back to Japan. This was analyzed by Kawade, who developed and perfected the technique (pl.49). In *shotai-jippo* an object is prepared for cloisonné enamelling, though often the wires are only fixed with glue. Importantly, the interior is not enamelled, thereby increasing the failure rate through stresses during the firing process. Once the piece has been completed, clear lacquer is applied to its polished exterior to protect it from the acid that is then used to dissolve the copper body. The result is an object consisting of semi-transparent panels of enamel held together by a pattern of fine wires. The popularity of *shotai-jippo* led to the technique being adopted by many other manufacturers (pl.50).

The Ando Company won many prizes at world exhibitions, starting with the 1893 World's Columbian Exposition in Chicago. Around 1900, it was appointed as an official supplier of cloisonné to the imperial household and although no craftsman was given the title of 'Imperial Craftsman', the Ando Company was the main provider of enamels for imperial gifts. Furthermore, the Ando Company is unique in that it is the only manufacturer with its roots in the Golden Age that is still producing high-quality cloisonné enamels today.

Until its closure in the 1990s, the Inaba Company of Kyoto was another survivor from the Golden Age. It was founded in 1886 by Inaba Isshin, a former samurai who had started working in enamels in 1875 to supplement his meagre stipend. His art name, Nanaho, is a play on the word *shippo*, the characters for which can be also be read as Nanaho. The company's output was rather eclectic: it combined designs and techniques used by other Kyoto makers together with those of Nagoya manufacturers, particularly Ando and Hayashi Kodenji (pls. 54 and 55). The third and fourth generation heads of the family, Inaba Katsumi and Inaba Hiroyuki, still live in Kyoto and are invaluable sources of information about the history of cloisonné making in Japan. The family's archives, together with tools and enamelling materials, are preserved in the Museum of Kyoto and the Kyoto Municipal Museum of Art (pl.56).

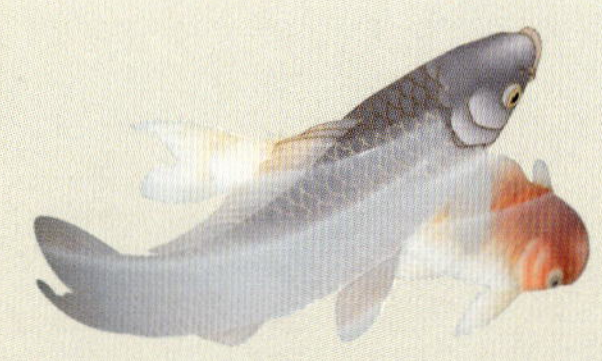

Design for a cloisonné vase, attributed to Namikawa Yasuyuki, from 'Historical Examples of the Progress of Modern Industrial Art in Japan as shown in the Kyoto Exhibition, Meiji 32, 4th month', published by the Ministry of Agriculture and Commerce, Commercial Crafts Bureau, 1900.

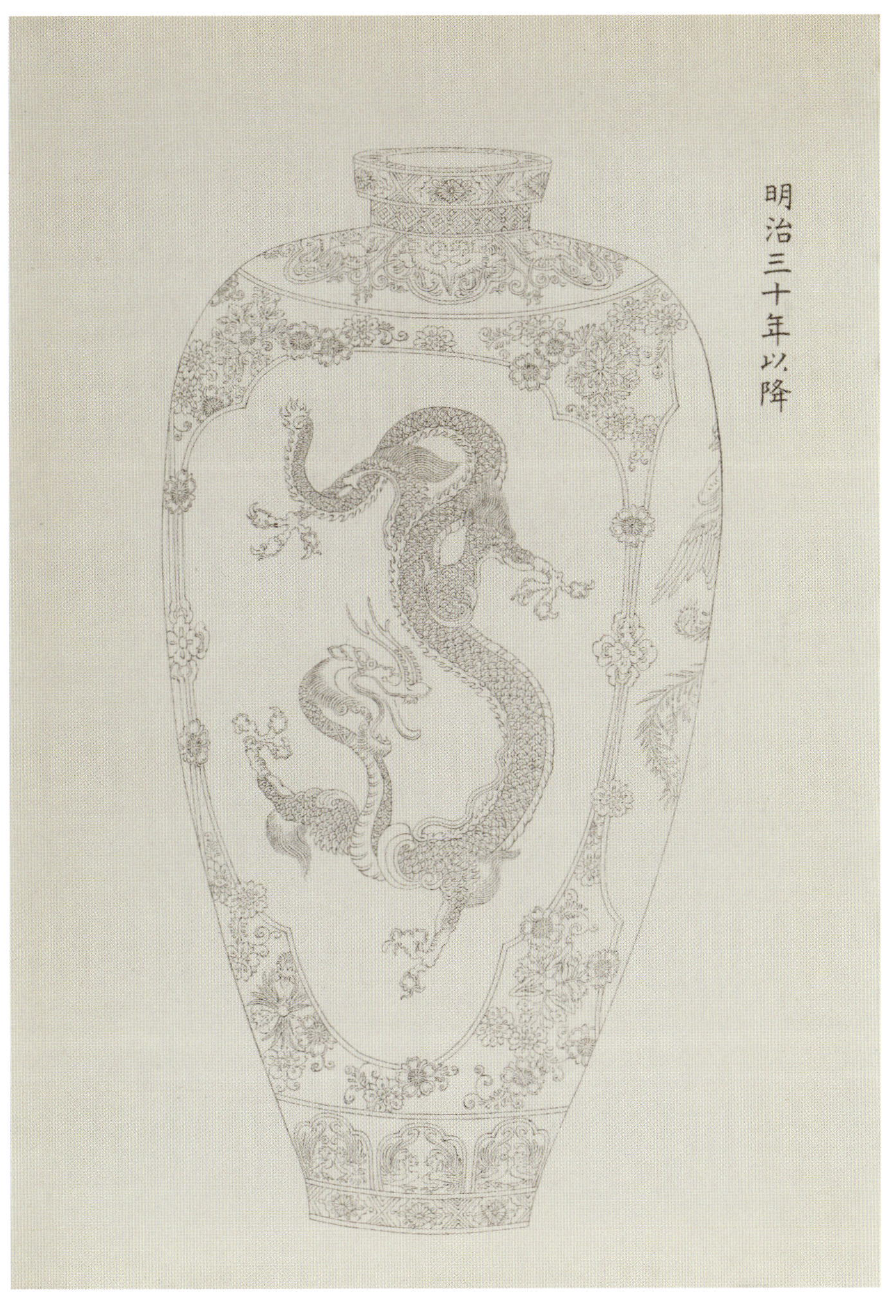

28

Vase decorated with
silver and gold wire
and an enamel design
of birds and flowers,
including a flowering
magnolia, all on a
black ground; the
shoulder has alternating
butterflies and flowers
on a brown enamel
ground.

Signed on an applied
silver tablet 'Kyoto
Namikawa [Yasuyuki]',
Kyoto, *c.*1890.

Height 13cm,
width 6cm.

29

Vase with ground
of alternating panels of
blue-black and speckled
aventurine green
enamels overlaid with
a design of flowers,
karakusa scrolls and
butterflies.

Signed on an applied
silver tablet 'Kyoto
Namikawa [Yasuyuki]',
Kyoto, *c.*1890.

Height 10cm,
width 5.5cm.

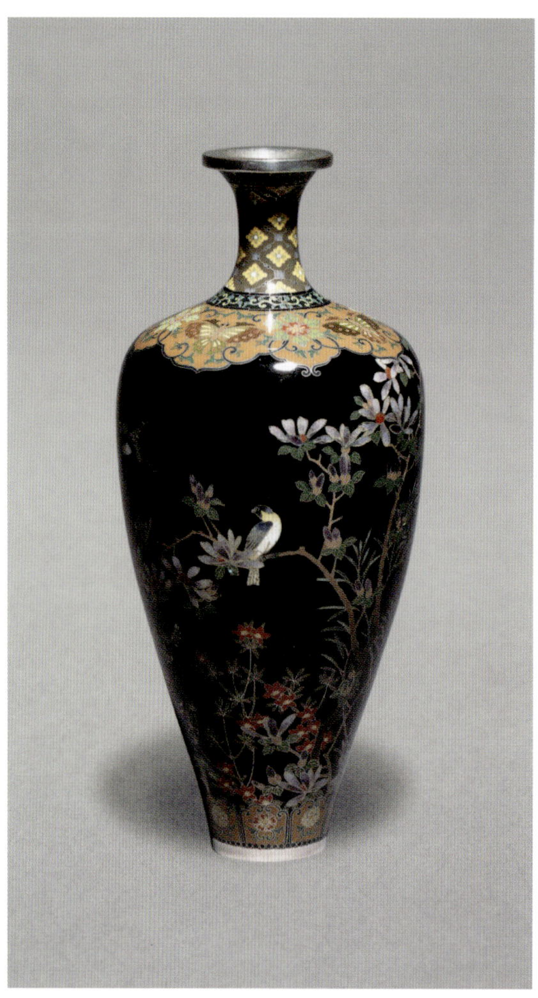

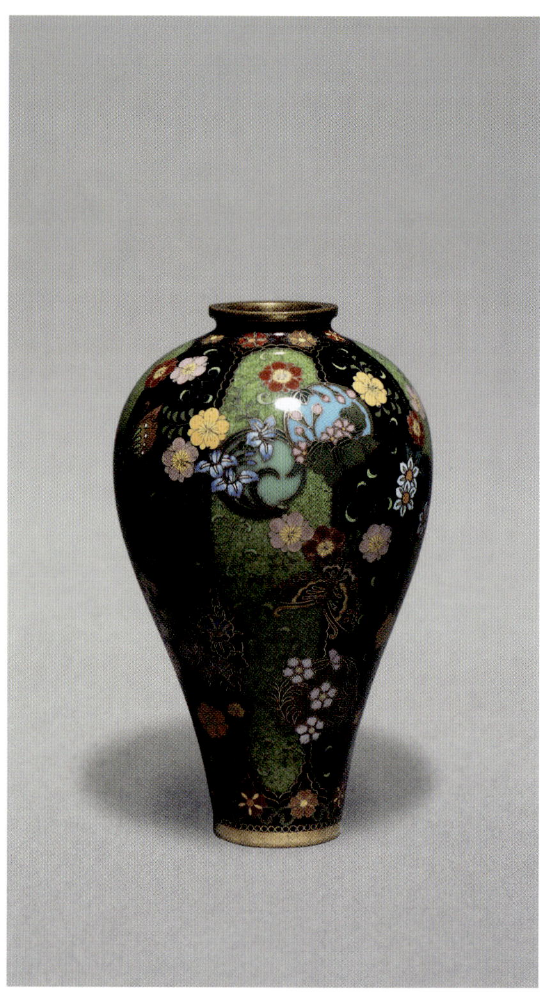

30

Detail from stereograph no.69: 'Expert workmen creating exquisite designs in cloisonné, Mr Namikawa in the background, Kyoto, Japan'.

Underwood & Underwood, 1904.

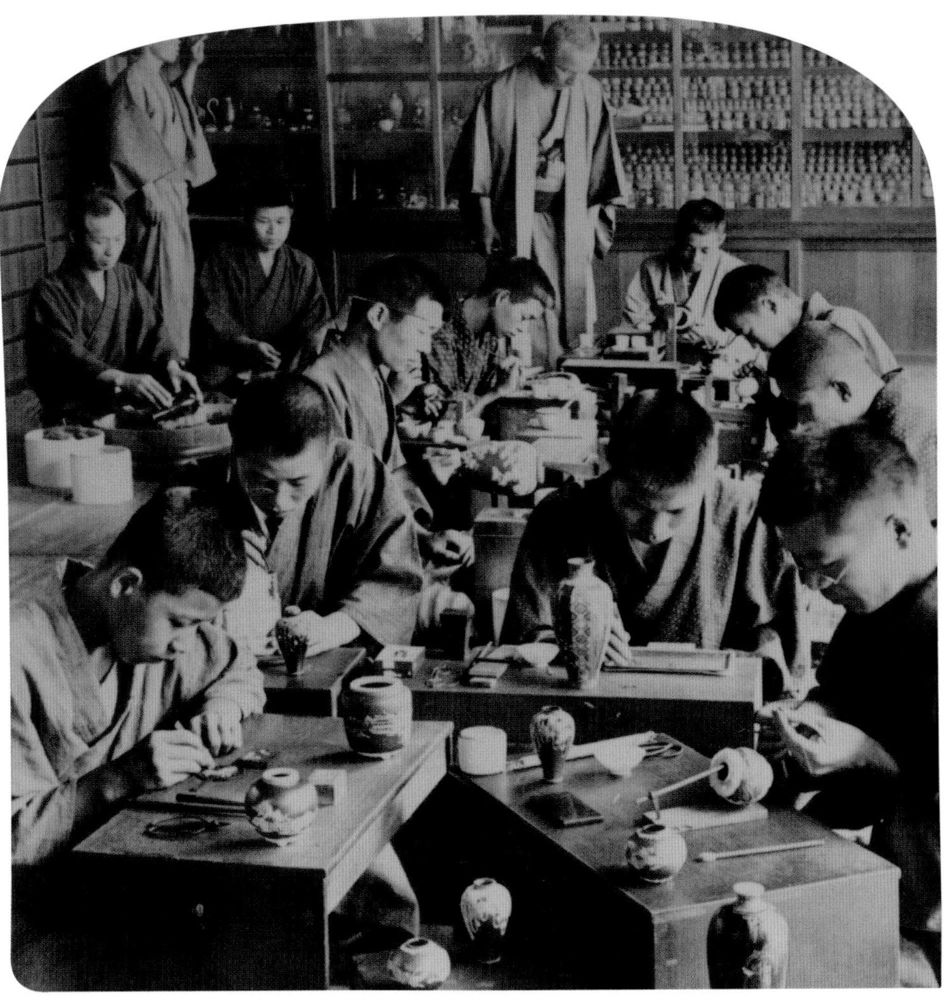

31

Lidded vase with black
enamel ground and
three panels of speckled
brown enamel containing,
respectively, a stylized
dragon, a *ho-o* bird,
peonies and butterflies.

Signed on an applied silver
tablet 'Kyoto Namikawa
[Yasuyuki]', Kyoto, *c.* 1890.

Height 10cm, width 8cm.

32

Dish decorated with a
butterfly in silver and gold
wire in a cream enamel
roundel surrounded
by stylized scrolling
chrysanthemums and
larch leaves on a black
enamel ground.

Unsigned but attributed
to Namikawa Yasuyuki,
Kyoto, *c.* 1890.

Diameter 13cm.

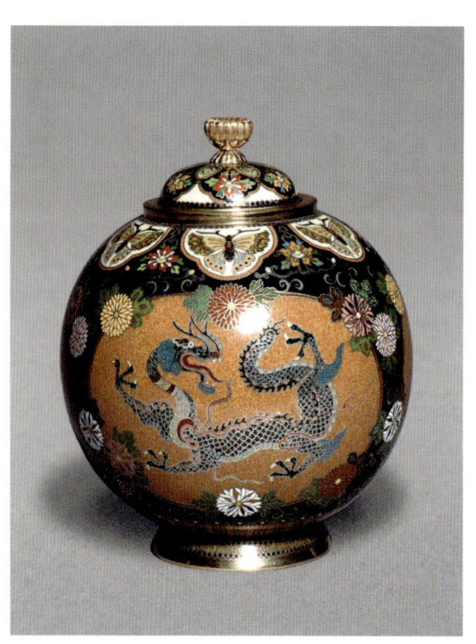

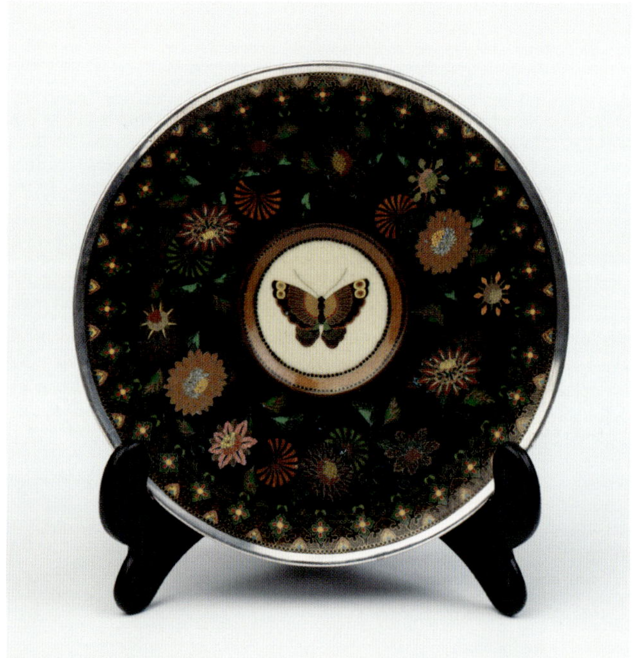

33

Group of lidded vases, decorated with butterflies and summer and early autumn flowers. The theme continues on the opposite side of the two smaller vases, while on the larger vase there is a superbly fashioned *ho-o* bird.

Engraved signature 'Kyoto Namikawa zo' on the larger vase and 'Namikawa zo' on the others, Kyoto, *c.*1880–90.

Height (left and right) 11cm, width 6cm; height (centre) 14cm, width 9.5cm.

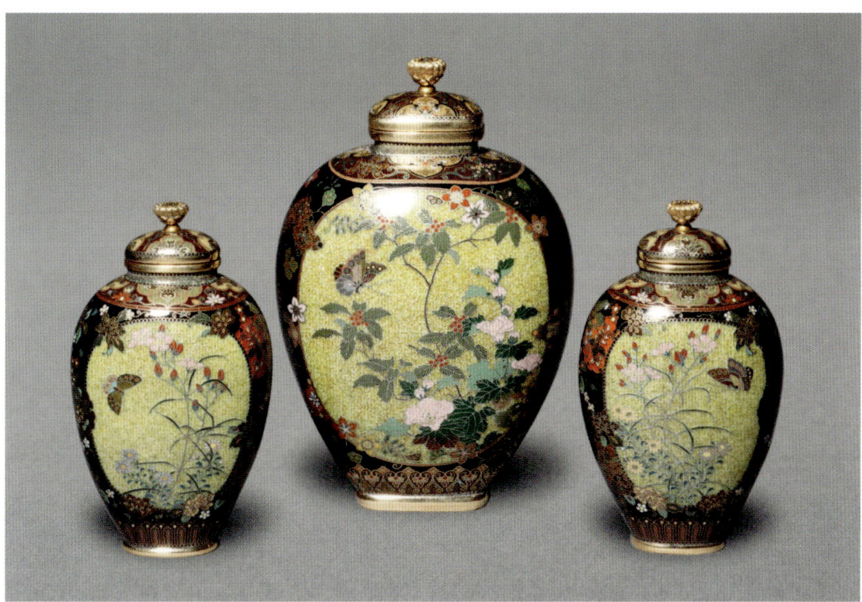

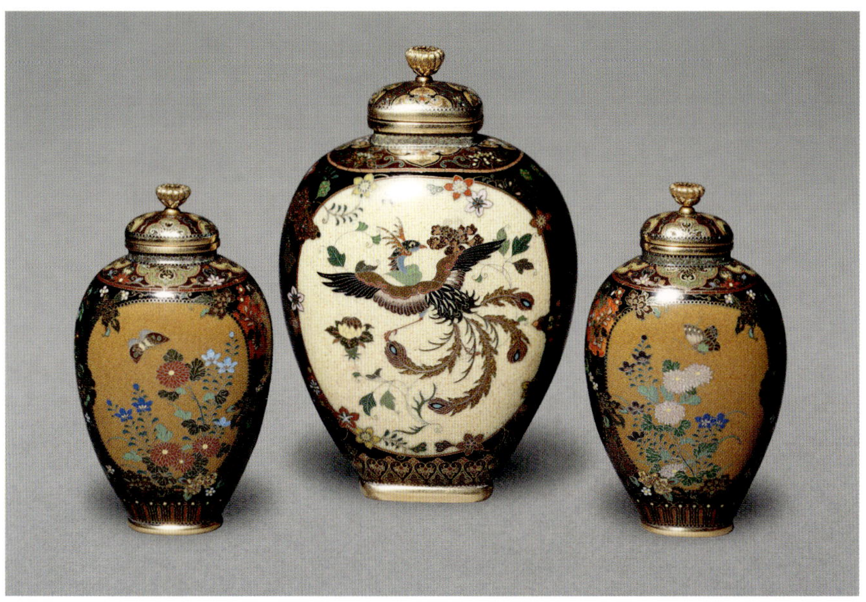

34

Vase with turquoise
enamel ground decorated
with chrysanthemums,
hydrangeas, gentians
and irises in silver wire
and polychrome-shaded
enamels; the flowers
represent all the seasons
except winter.

Signed on an applied silver
tablet 'Kyoto Namikawa
[Yasuyuki]', Kyoto,
*c.*1875–80.

Height 10.5cm, width 5cm.

35

Vase with brass-wire
decoration of a bird,
possibly a Java sparrow,
on a flowering plum
branch.

Signed on an applied
silver tablet 'Kyoto
Namikawa [Yasuyuki]',
Kyoto, *c.*1900–10.

Height 15cm, width 5cm.

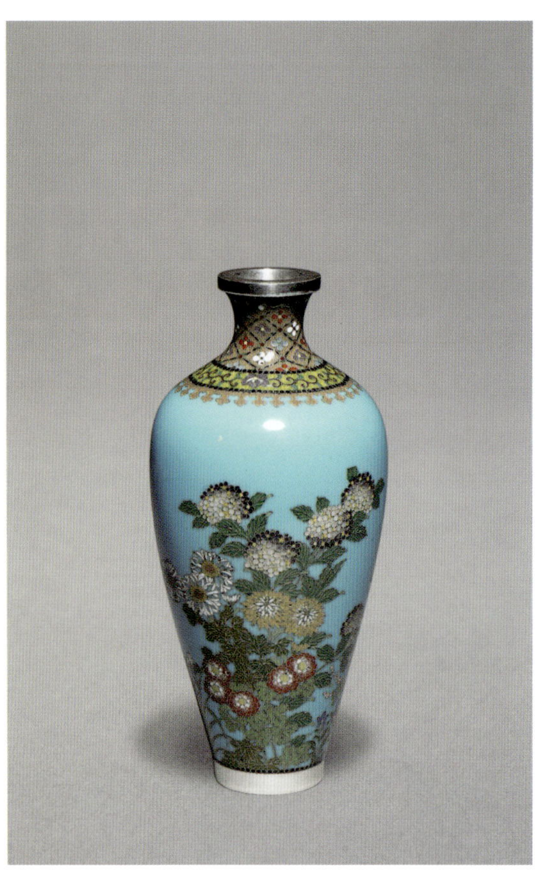

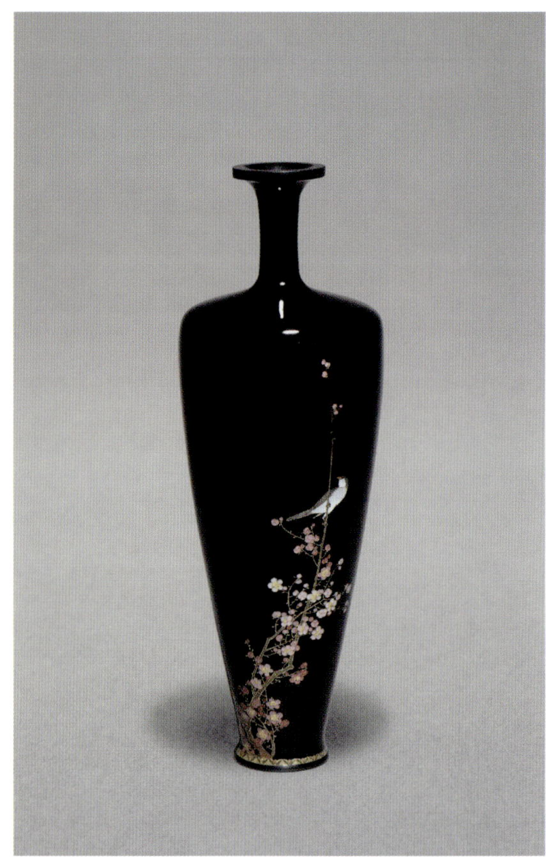

Pair of vases with a pale grey enamel ground typical of Namikawa Sosuke, with an elegant design of flowering chrysanthemums.

'*Sakigake*' seal of Namikawa Sosuke, Tokyo, *c.* 1900.

Height 15.5cm, width 9.5cm.

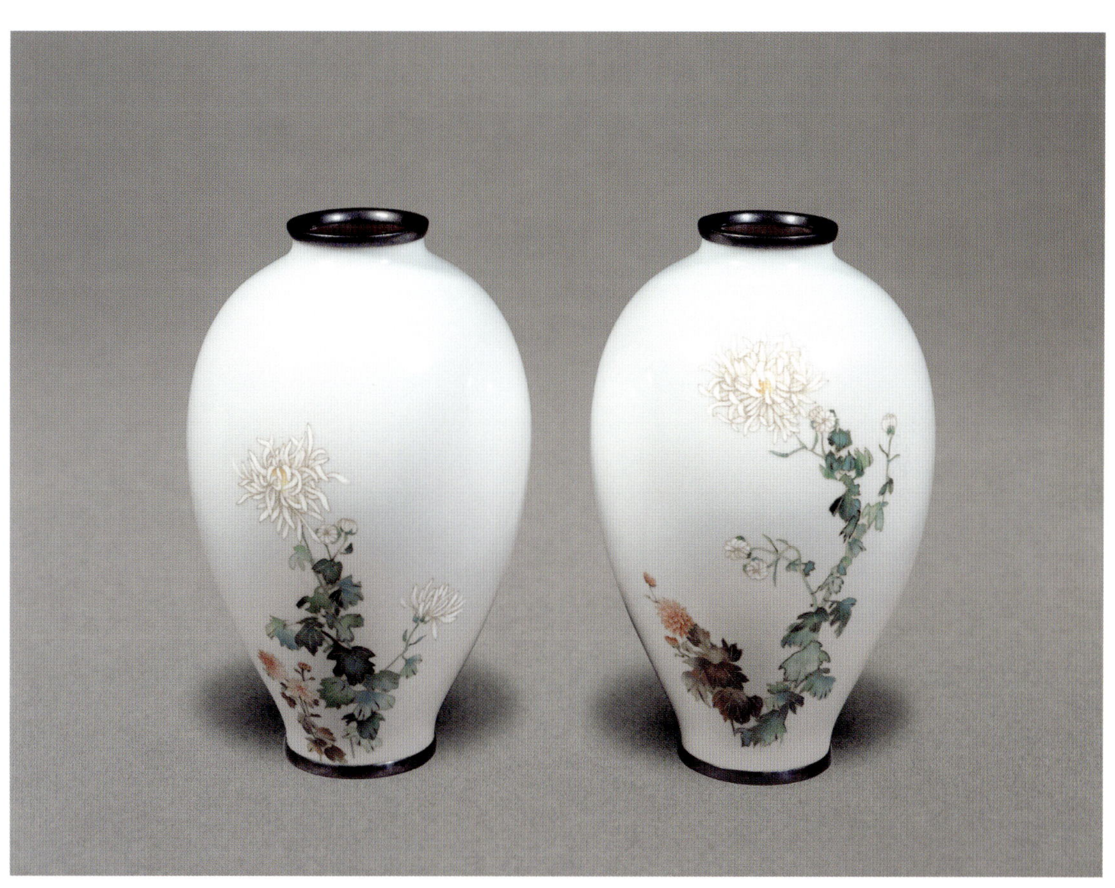

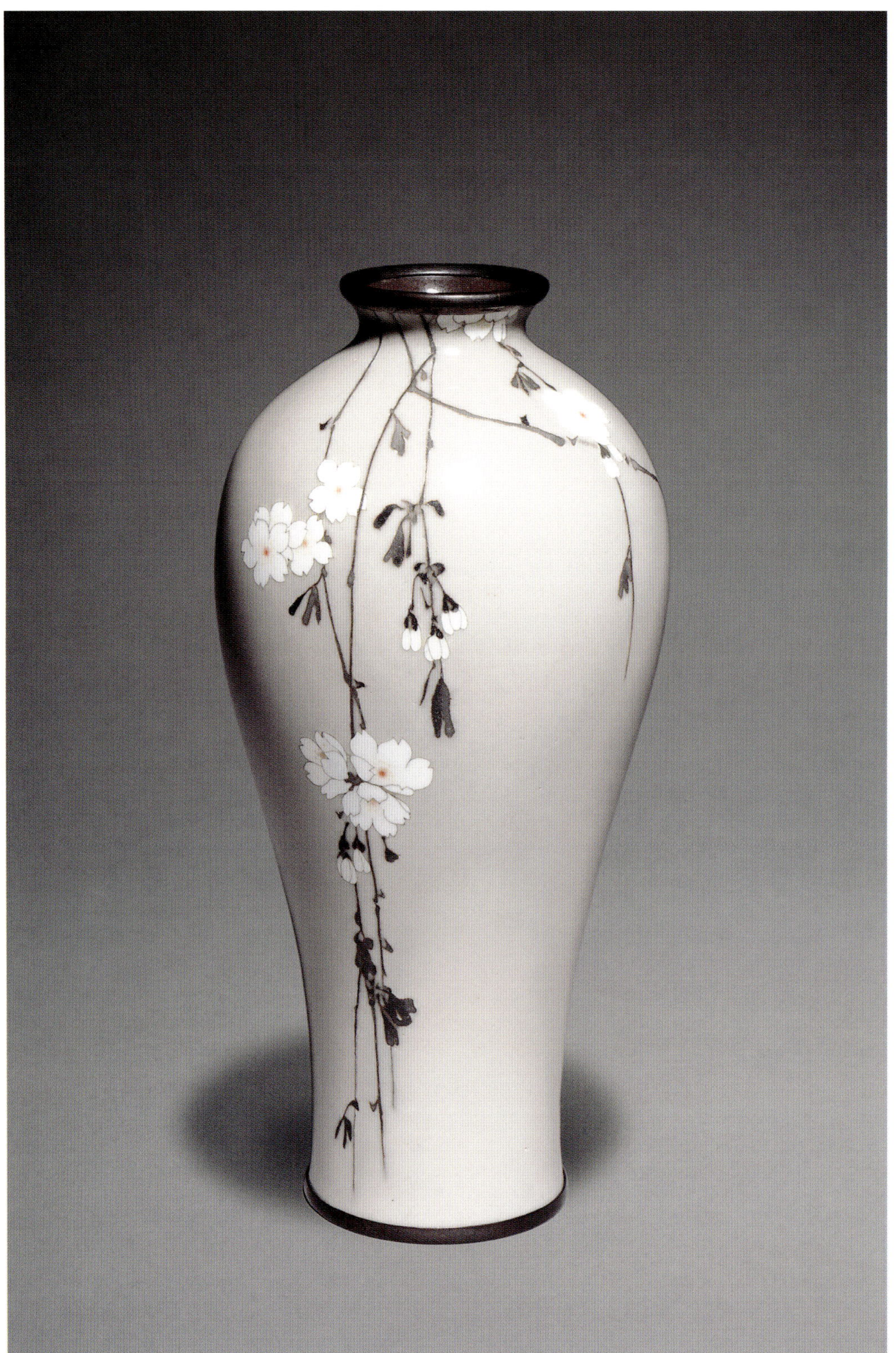

37

Vase with gold-wire and enamel design of hanging cherry blossom (*Hidare Zakura*) in shades of white, pink and grey on a warm-grey enamel ground.

'*Sakigake*' seal of Namikawa Sosuke, Tokyo, *c.*1900.

Height 19cm, width 8.5cm.

38

Pair of vases decorated in ginbari enamels with carp and pondweed on a *nanako* background.

Mark '[Ogasawara] Shuzo', Nagoya, *c.*1900–10.

Height 12cm, width 7.5cm.

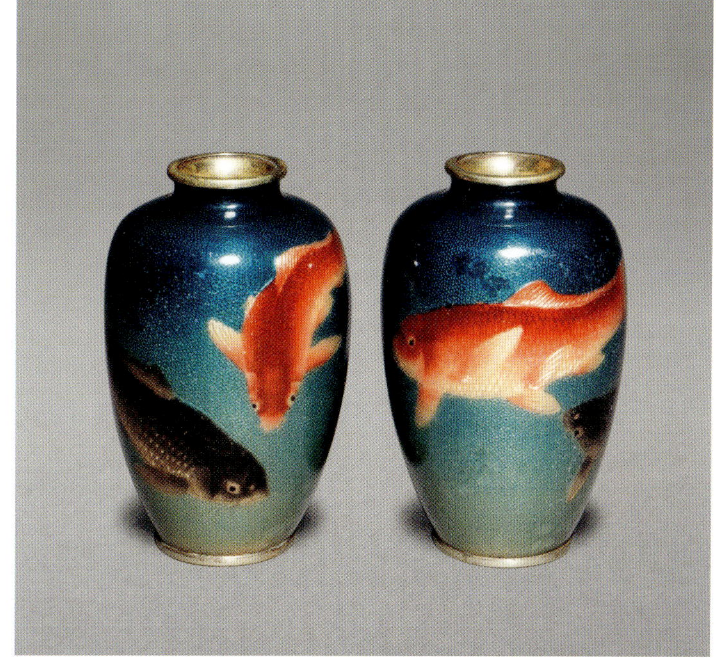

39

Pair of vases with a design of tethered hawks on rails decorated with a wood-grain effect, from which hang curtains with a scrolling flower design.

Impressed mark on the base 'Ota [Jinnoei]' inside the outline of an incense burner, Nagoya, *c.*1880–85.

Height 12.5cm, width 5.5cm.

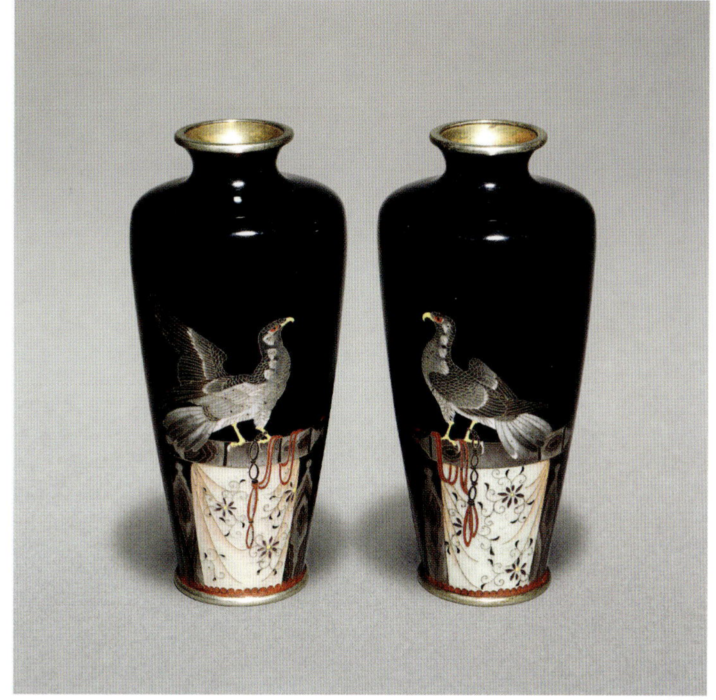

40

Tazza with cream
enamel ground
decorated with a *ho-o*
bird in gold wire with
a triple paulownia-leaf
design in silver wire and
translucent *totai-jippo*
enamels. The central
white butterfly is an
as yet unidentified
family crest.

Mark of Gonda Hirosuke,
Nagoya, *c.* 1912–26.

Height 12.5cm,
diameter 24.5cm.

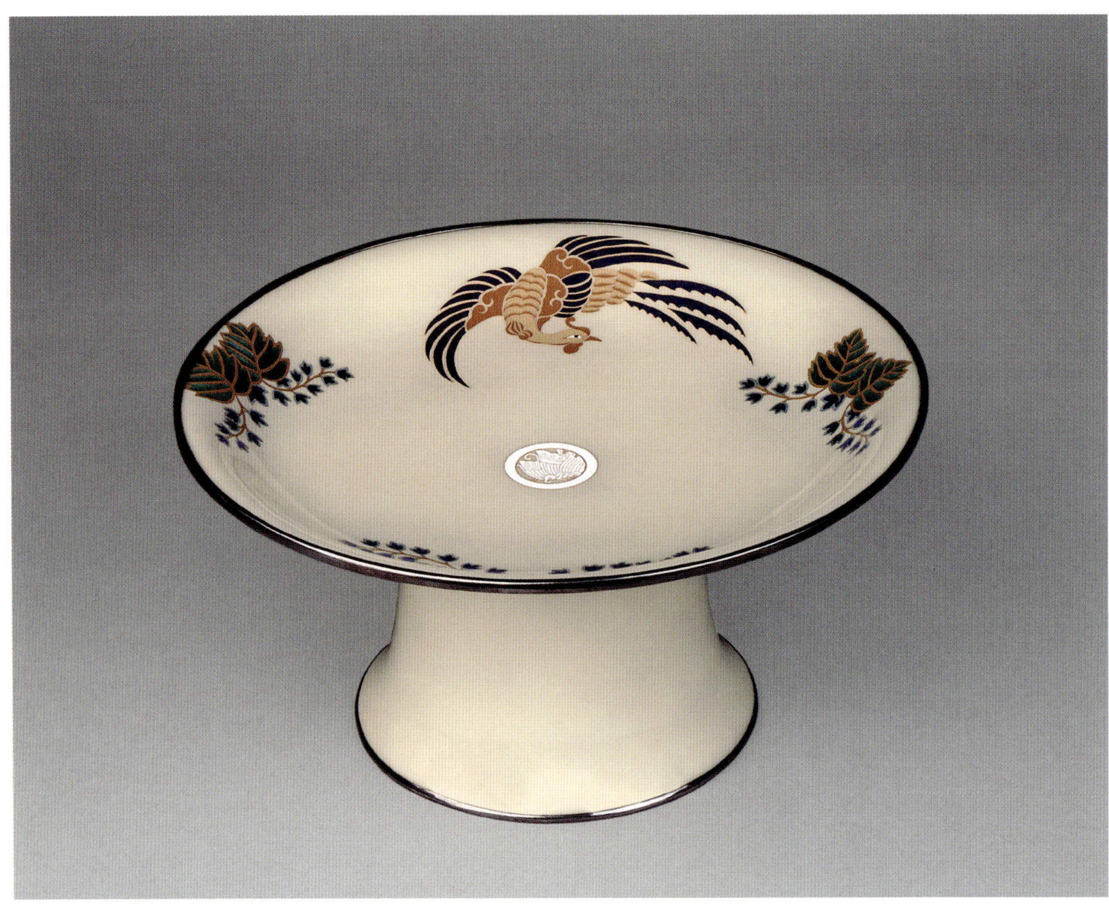

41

Box decorated with a
flower arrangement
in a woven basket and
representing the four
seasons, sections of
vine and plum blossom
continue from the lid
across the rim onto
the main body.

Seal 'Kawade
[Shibataro]', inside a
double gourd, Nagoya,
*c.*1900–12.

Height 5cm,
width 12cm.

42

Pair of vases with design
of little grey and white
moriage-enamelled egrets
on a ground of *flambé*-
style enamel.

Signed 'Hattori
[Tadasaburo]', Nagoya,
*c.*1900–10.

Height 12cm,
width 6.5cm.

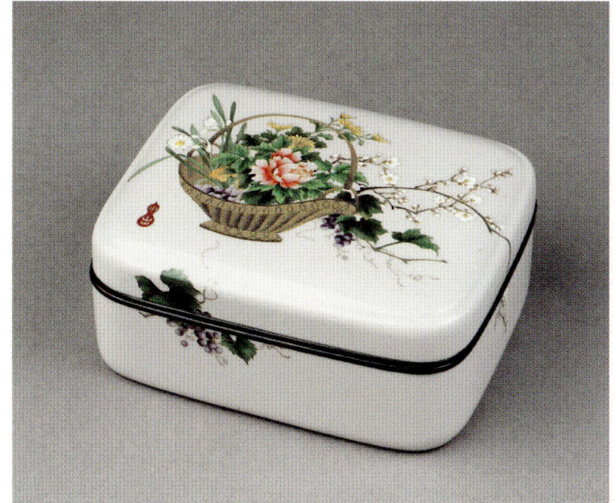

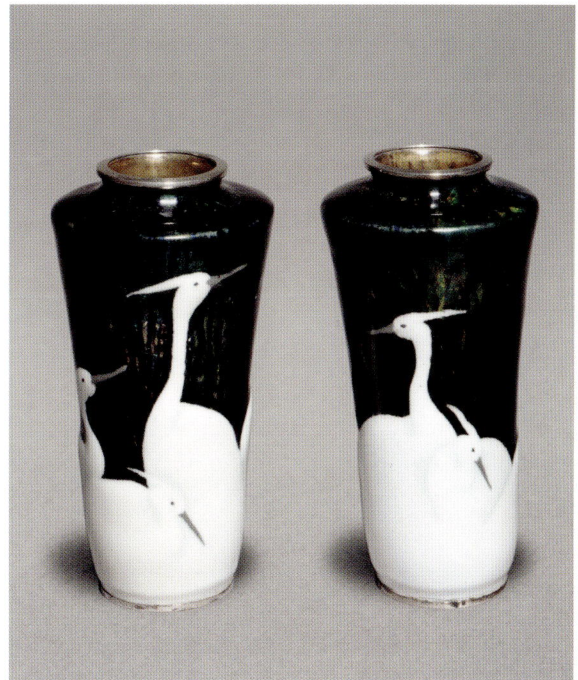

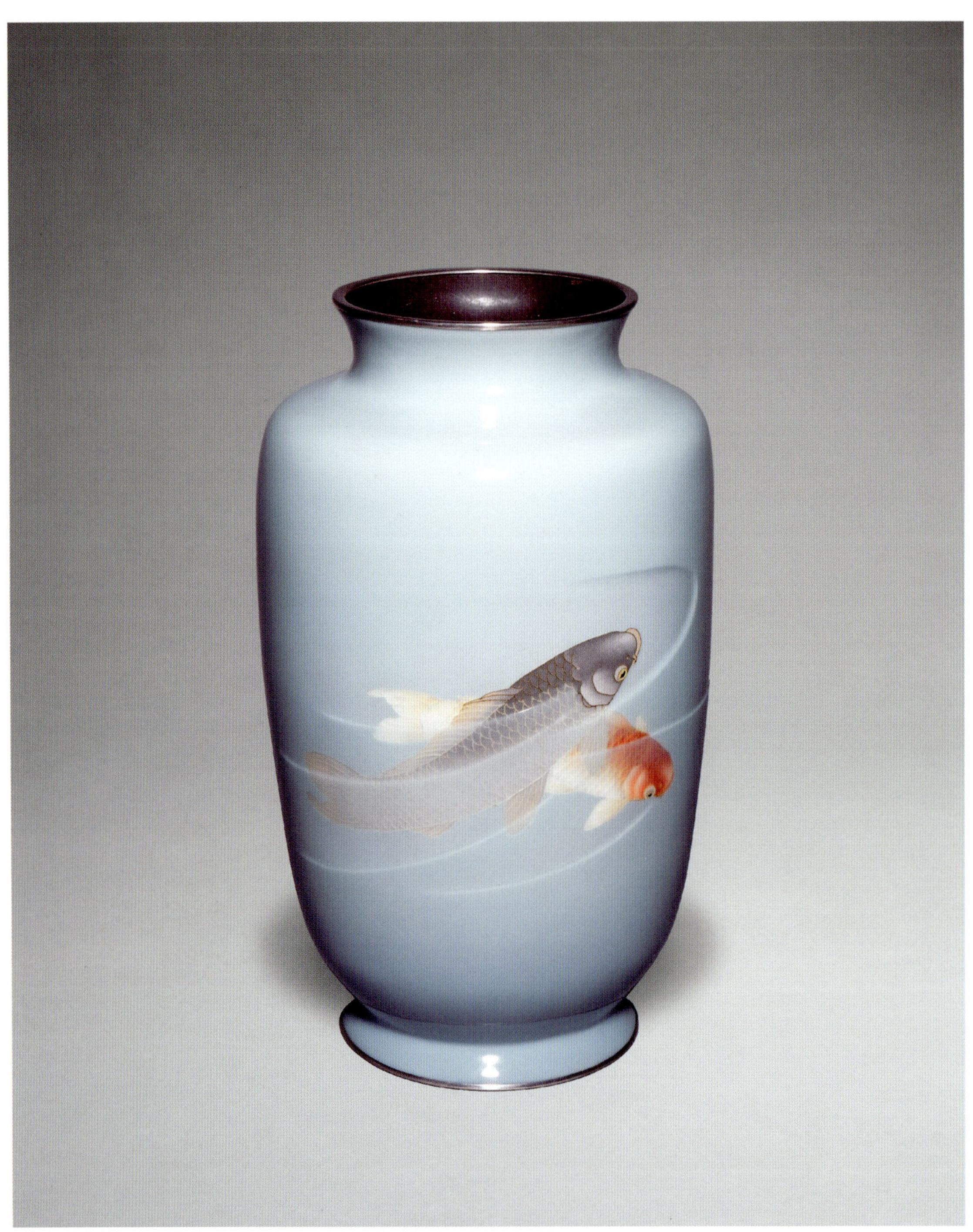

43
Vase with a pale
blue enamel ground
decorated with three
carp swimming
through *moriage*
ripples; areas of the
fish are covered with
clear enamel, which
emphasizes the head
emerging to create
a ripple.

Unsigned, probably
the Ando Company,
Nagoya, *c.*1905–10.

Height 30cm,
width 18cm.

44
Vase with graduated
peach-coloured
enamel ground,
decorated with a
marsh plant of the
type commonly
known as arrowhead;
the twisting of the
leaves adds to the
naturalistic design.

Mark of the Ando
Company, Nagoya,
*c.*1900–10.

Height 24.5cm,
width 11cm.

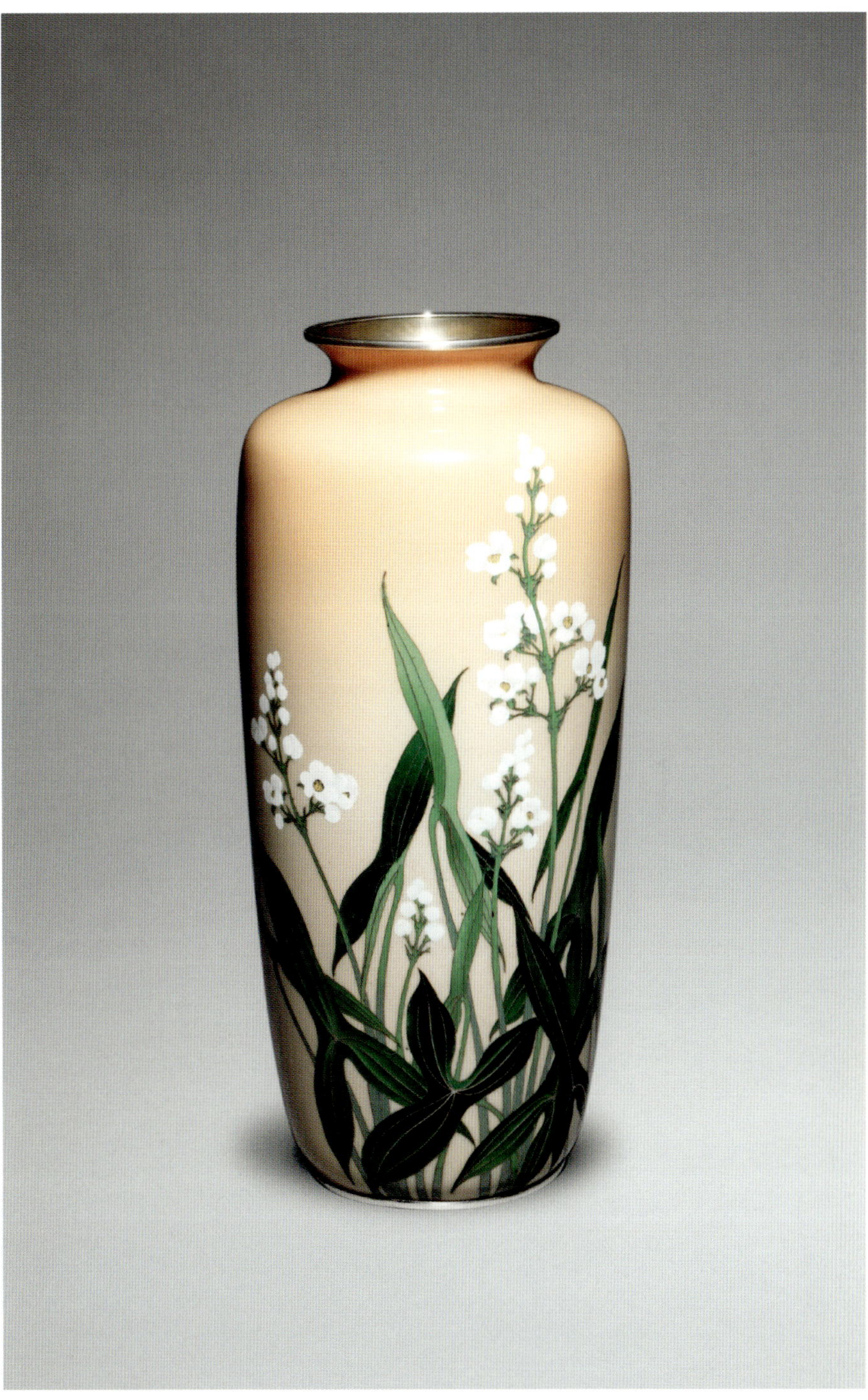

45

Vase with shaded
peach-coloured
enamel ground,
decorated in brass and
silver wire with two
Java sparrows flying
above maple trees in
early autumn.

Mark of the Ando
Company, Nagoya,
*c.*1900–10.

Height 29.5cm,
width 10.5cm.

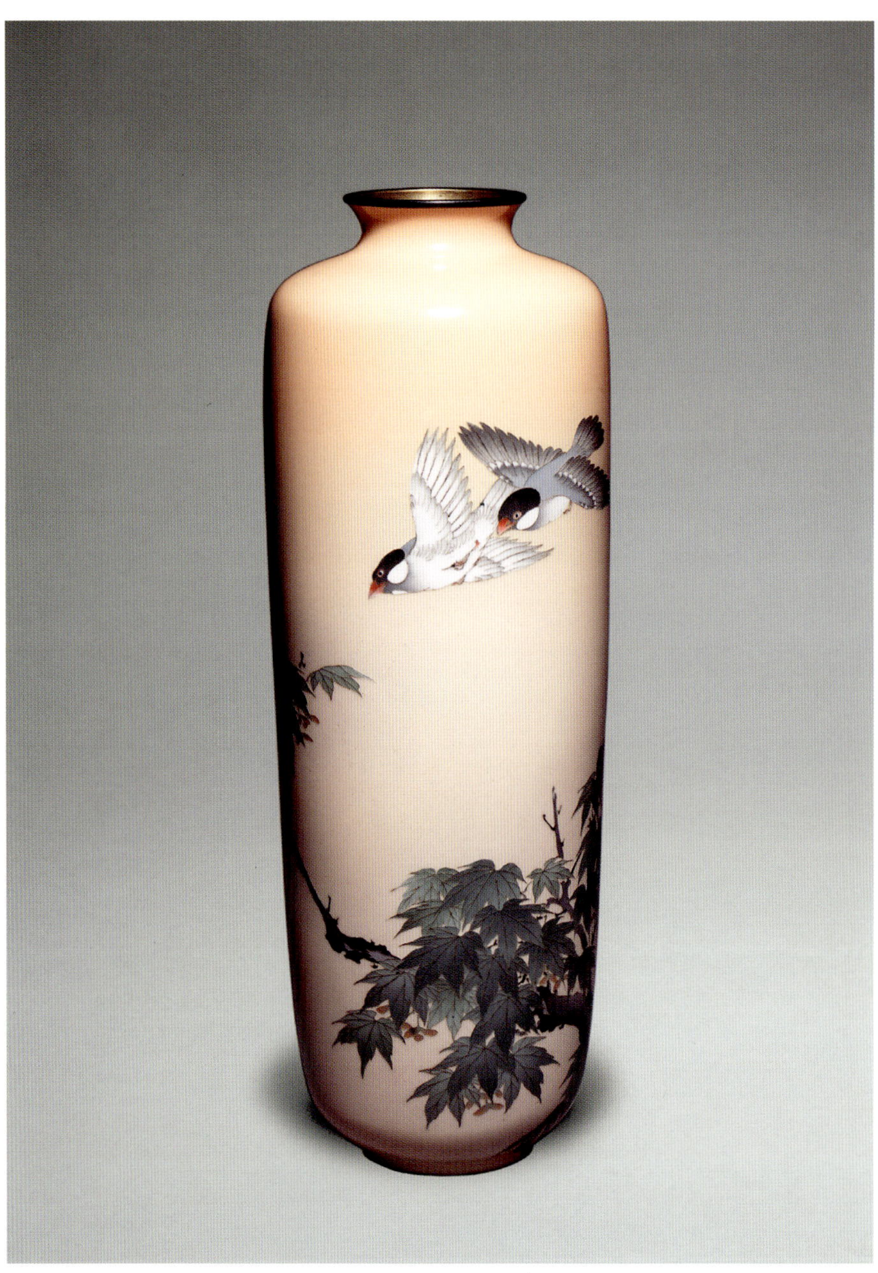

46

Vase with deep blue
enamel ground,
decorated with
flowering and trailing
paulownia (*kiri*)
in silver wire and
translucent *totai-jippo*
enamels in shades of
orange, white and
purple.

Mark of the Ando
Company, Nagoya,
*c.*1910–20.

Height 24cm,
width 14cm.

47

Vase with a dull
beige enamel ground
decorated in silver
wire and shaded white
and green enamel
orchids with details in
low *moriage*. A wasp
delineated in gold
wire hovers near the
flowers.

Unsigned, possibly
the Ando Company,
Nagoya, *c.*1912–26.

Height 28cm,
width 19cm.

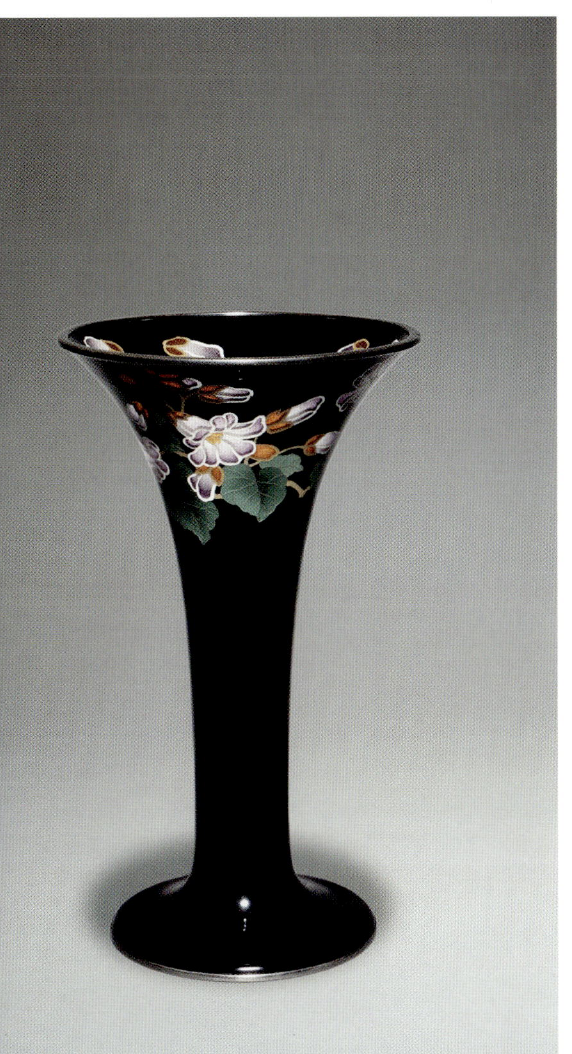

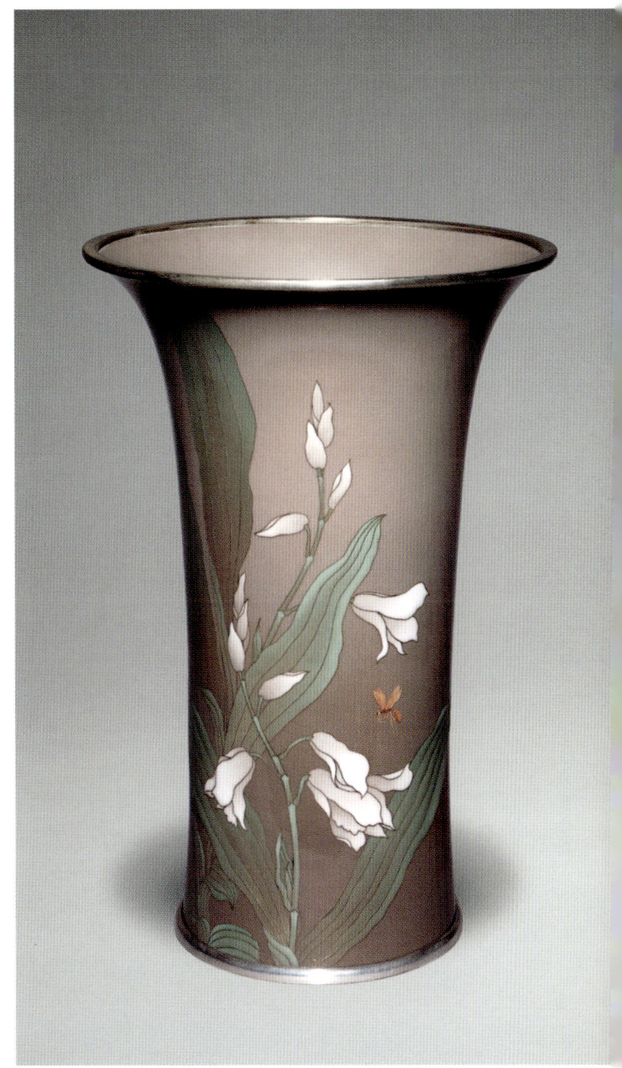

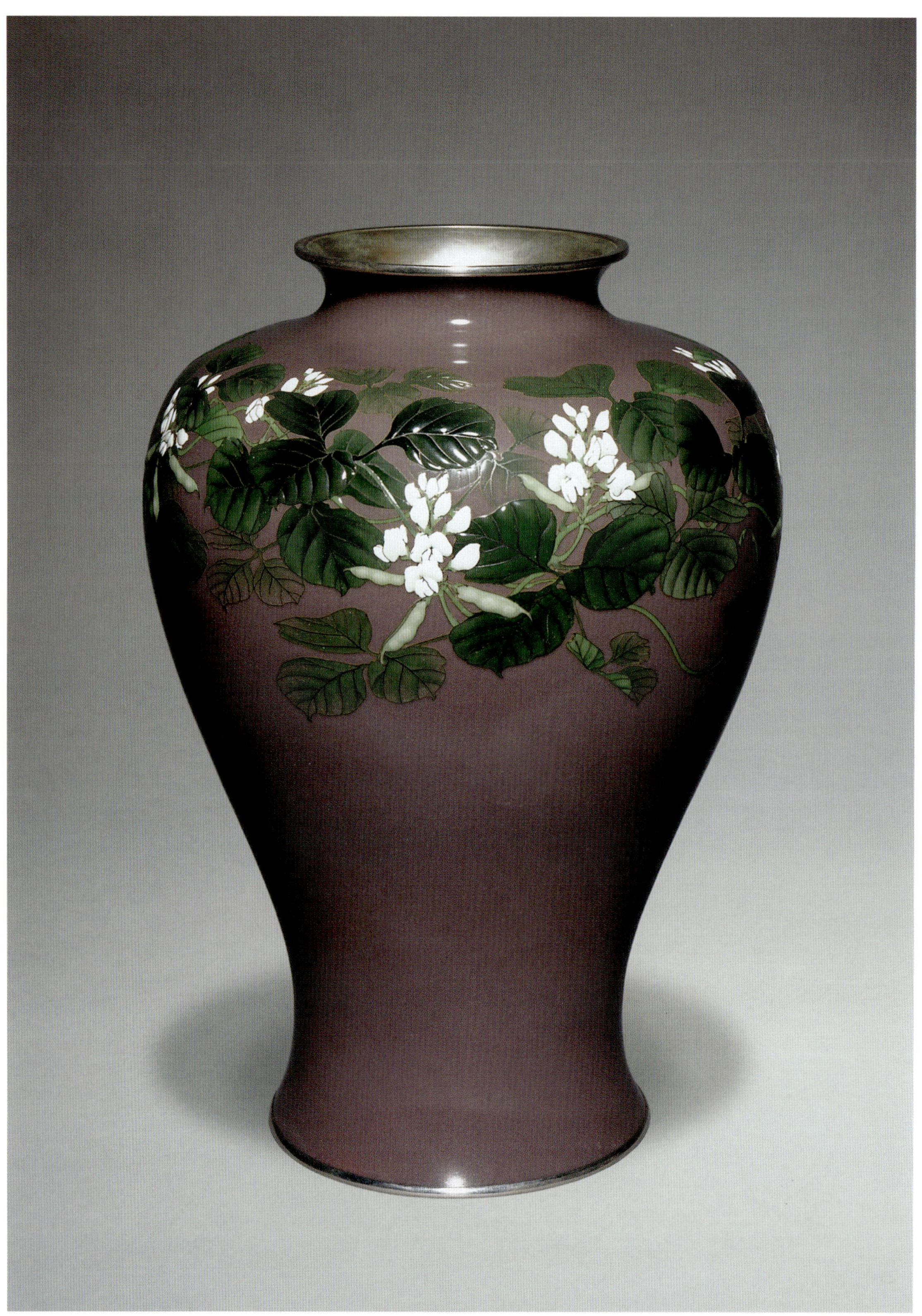

48
Vase with semi-matt pale aubergine enamel ground decorated with a trailing and flowering legume in *moriage* enamels, which create a naturalistic, almost three-dimensional composition.

Mark of the Ando Company, Nagoya, 1912–26.

Height 30cm, width 20cm.

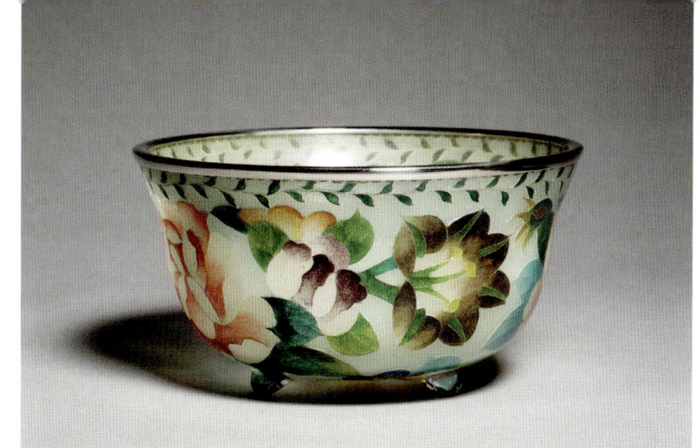

49
Bowl with a silver-wire design of peonies, convolvulus, roses, gentians and chrysanthemums in polychrome-shaded *shotai-jippo* enamels on a pale green ground.

Unsigned, Nagoya, 1912–26.

Height 7.5cm, width at rim 13.5cm.

50
Two vases in *shotai-jippo* enamels, one decorated with maple leaves, the other with cherry blossom, which represent autumn and spring respectively.

Unsigned, Nagoya, *c.*1926–89.

Height 9cm, width 8cm.

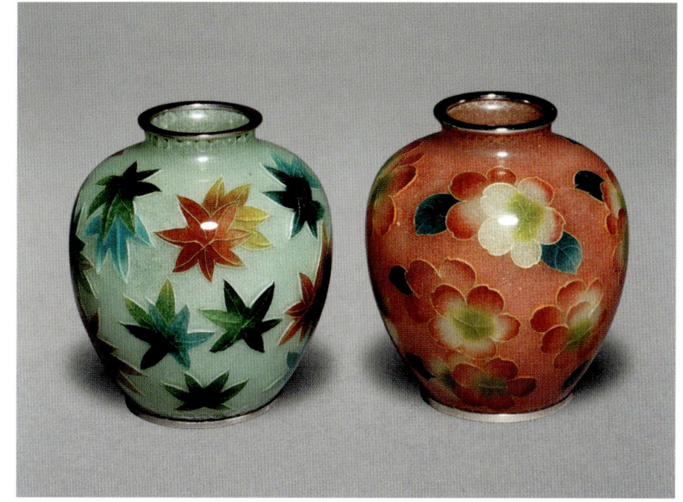

51
Vase with a body of hammered *nanako* ground and covered with a transparent red *akasuke* enamel; the lower part is decorated with a design of a dragon emerging from wild waves.

Mark of the Ando Company, Nagoya, *c.*1900.

Height 16.5cm, width 6cm.

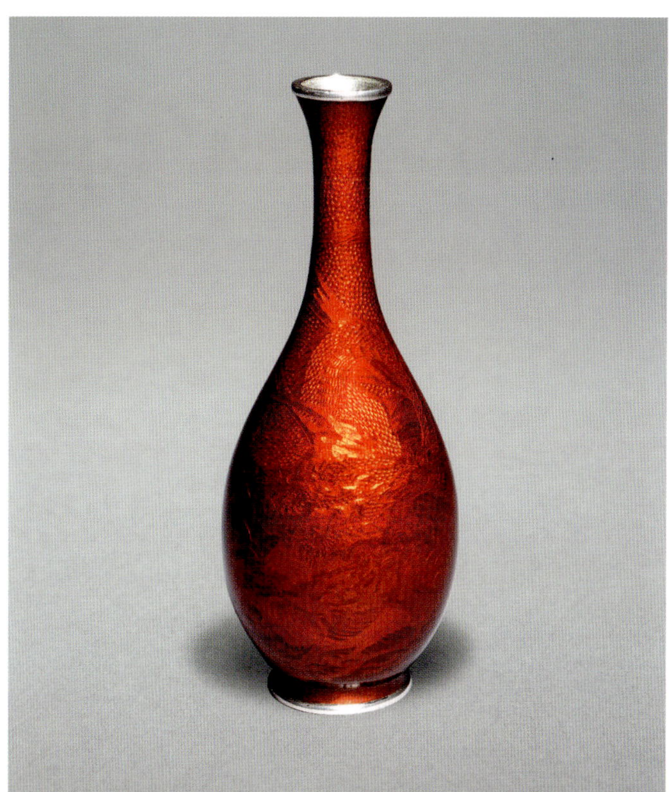

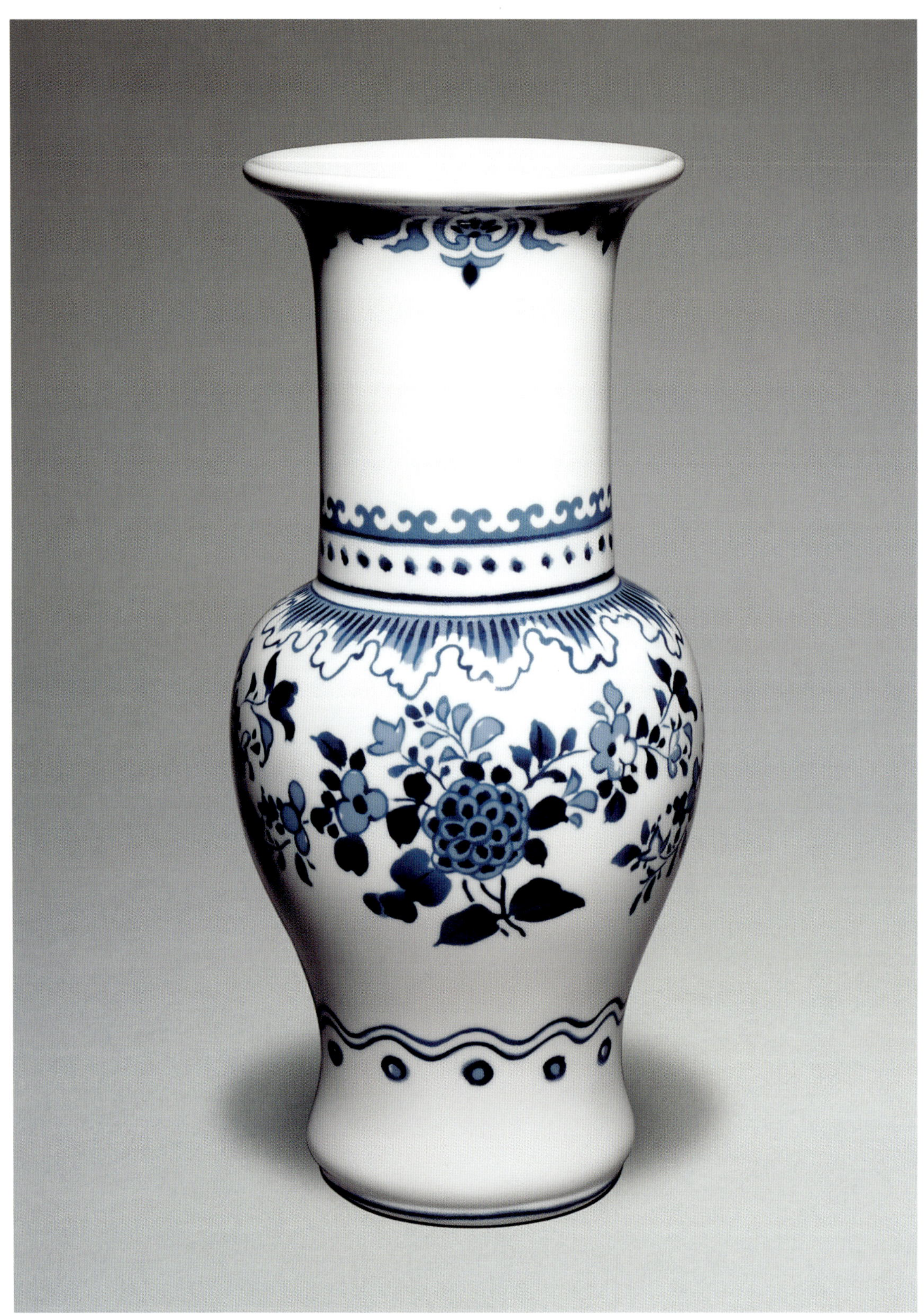

52

Vase enamelled in
blue and white floral
motifs and geometric
patterns. The shape,
palette and decoration
are reminiscent of
Dutch Delft pottery.

Mark of the Inaba
Company, Kyoto,
c.1912–20.

Height 31cm,
width 14cm.

53

Original photograph
of the Delft-style vase
in pl.52, c.1912–20.
From the archive
of Inaba Shichiho,
second-generation
maker, in the Kyoto
Municipal Museum.

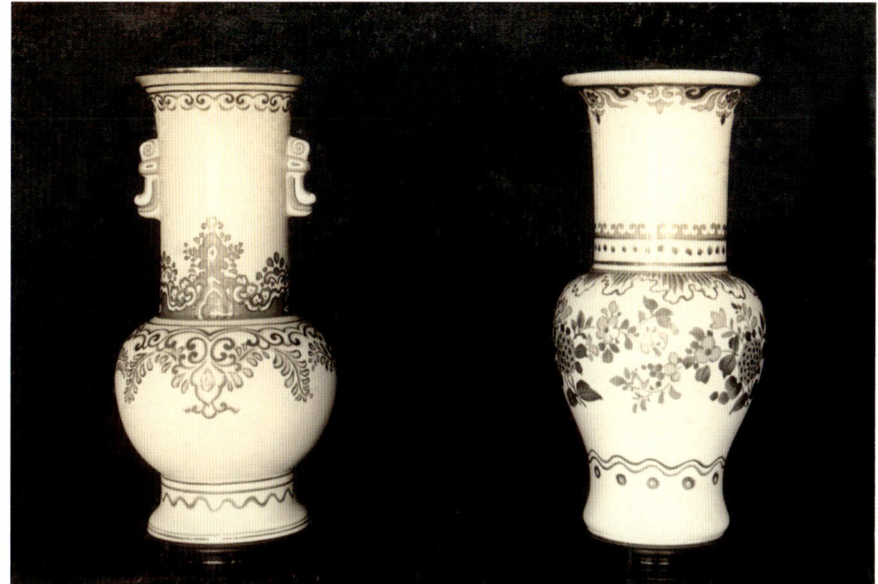

54
Dish with central
decoration of a *ho-o*
bird in shades of
green, blue and white
enamels, surrounded
by a stylized floral and
leaf pattern.

Mark of the Inaba
Company, Kyoto,
*c.*1912–26.

Height 6.5cm,
width 22.5cm.

55
Vase decorated
on a black enamel
ground with a tree
sparrow perched on a
flowering cherry. The
shape and decoration
of the vase are similar
to those produced by
Namikawa Yasuyuki,
whose workshop was
geographically very
close to that of Inaba.

Mark of the Inaba
Company, Kyoto,
*c.*1895–1910.

Height 12cm,
width 4.5cm.

56
Inaba Shichiho
standing before a
display of his work on
the upper floor of the
Inaba shop in Kyoto
*c.*1935–40. From
the archive of Inaba
Shichiho, second-
generation maker, in
the Kyoto Municipal
Museum.

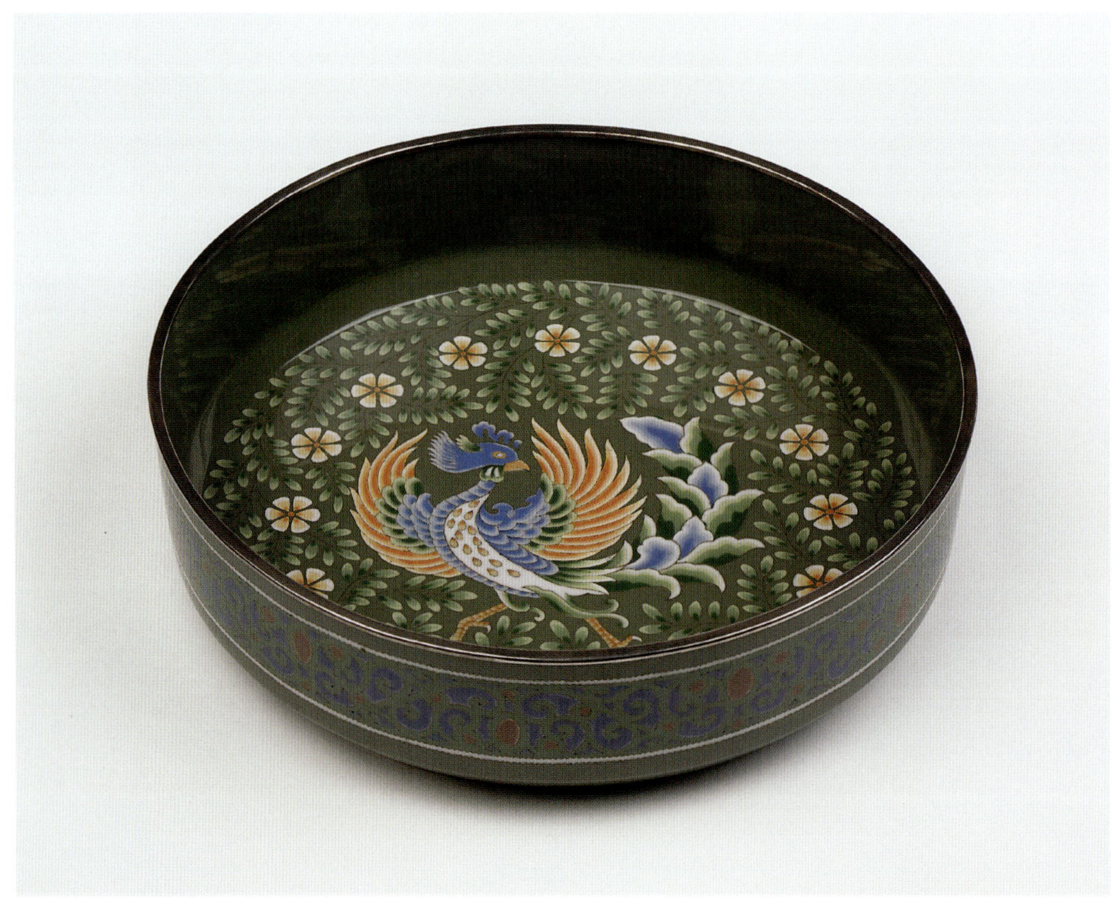

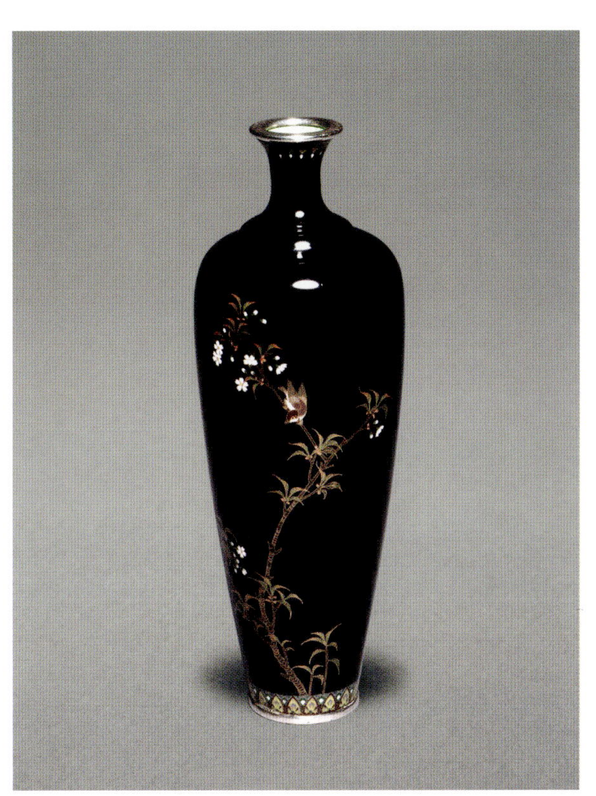

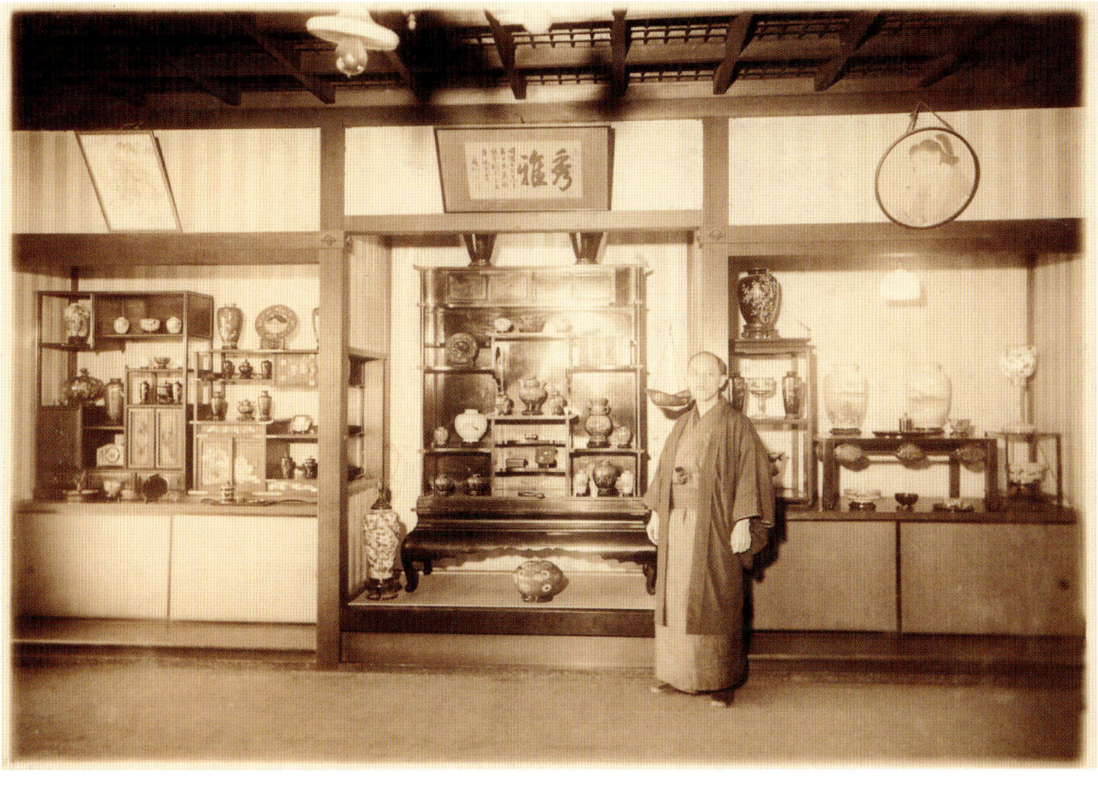

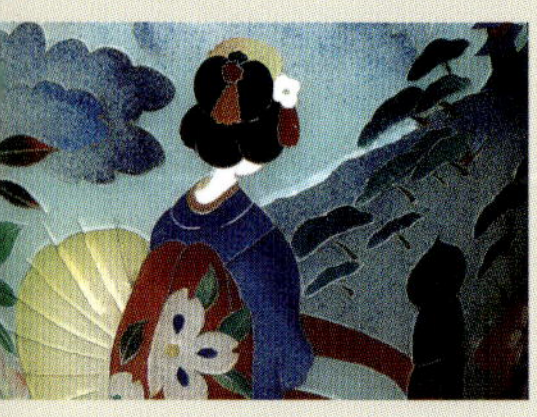

NEW MARKETS AND CHANGING TASTES: THE PRICE OF COMMERCIAL SUCCESS

It was some time before cloisonné enamels were deemed to have sufficient artistic merit to be in high demand in Japan itself, although the designation of the two Namikawa makers as Imperial Craftsmen no doubt provided a boost to domestic appreciation. Harada noted:

> It is only in comparatively recent years, most markedly within the last few years, that *shippo* began to find a place in Japanese homes as an ornament. As is so often the case with arts and crafts, there are two distinct types of enamel-work, one for foreign markets and the other for the home market... .
> (Harada, p.276)

So desirable was cloisonné as an art form that huge quantities of low-standard products had begun to flood the export market, causing interest in these wares to decline towards the end of the nineteenth century. As early as 1884 Bowes had commented:

> The modern enamels of Japan merit only a passing notice… At Yokohama, at Nagoya, in the province of Owari, and, I believe, at Kioto [*sic*] also, the industry is now carried on upon a large scale by native workmen, but mainly under French directors, who, studying what they suppose to be the requirements of the European market, have produced works deficient in beauty of form, colouring and workmanship.
> (Bowes 1884, pp.33–4)

The publicity brochure issued by Namikawa Sosuke some time after 1896 included extracts that further reflect on the circumstances around enamel production in Japan. In an article entitled 'Japanese Cloisonné: The great Namikawa, of Tokyo, describes the development of his art in the last two decades', Sosuke is quoted to have said:

I regret that the wide-spread demand for Japanese
products in your country has created an awkward
confusion and lack of discrimination as to what should
be classed as commercial commodities purely and what
should be given rank as aesthetic creations.

It is clear that by 1896 the production of export enamels from
Japan had become the victim of its own success. An almost
overwhelming demand for enamels resulting in the production of cheaper wares purely for export had gained the craft a
reputation for cheapness and shoddiness. This, combined with
overproduction, resulted in a decline in the industry that was
almost as rapid as its ascent. Harada later observed:

The *shippo* industry is already suffering a heavy penalty
– at least that class of ware which depended solely upon
the capricious demand of the West co-existent with
ignorance of the Japanese and their ideals. Let us take as
an illustration the case of Toshima, a village a few miles
from Nagoya. It is known properly by another name,
that of *Shippo Mura*, which means 'village of cloisonné
wares'… But nearly all the kilns in Toshima are now idle
and their workshops closed, while the annual output of
Japanese cloisonné has dwindled during the last six years
[1905–11] to less than one-third of what it used to be. The
appearance of the village was almost unbearable to the
writer when he visited it nearly two years ago... it is our
belief that the keynote tragedy lies in the misconception
of Western needs and the flooding of Western markets
with cheap, low-class wares.
(Harada, pp.278–81)

However, high-quality cloisonné enamels continued to be
produced for the imperial household, and the major companies, active after 1920 (chiefly Ando and Inaba), had a reliable
domestic market with much of their output catering for purely
Japanese taste while acknowledging art trends from outside
Japan (pls 65, 71). In 1957, the technique of cloisonné enamelling was selected as an 'Intangible Cultural Property for which
documentation and other measures should be taken'. The types
of work being produced today and exhibited in the annual
Nihon Dento Kogeiten (Exhibition of Japanese Traditional Art
Crafts) tend to be rather traditional in terms of technique and
form, although some modern makers are producing highly
innovative and challenging enamelled works (pl.74).

57

Vase with decoration of an *oiran* (high-class courtesan) and her attendant on a black enamel ground. The silver plate applied to the base is inscribed 'Kyoto Shibata'.

There has been much unresolved debate as to the relationship between Shibata and Namikawa Yasuyuki; Shibata's work can be confused with that of Yasuyuki and his seal was also very similar.

Kyoto, *c.* 1900–10.

Height 24.4cm.

Margary Gift

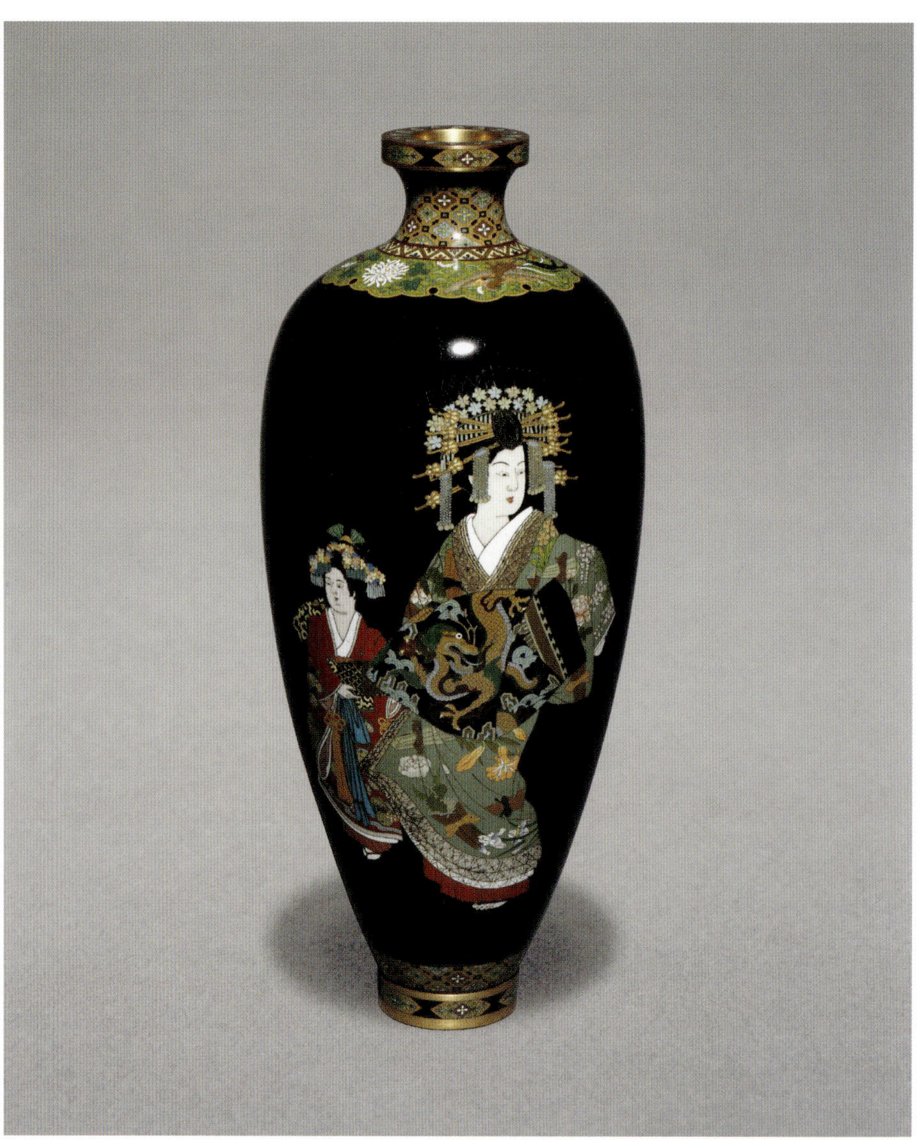

58

Document box decorated all over with chrysanthemums, flowers and *karakusa* with a gilt interior and silver handle in the form of a butterfly. The shape copies lacquer boxes of earlier periods.

Unsigned, Nagoya, *c.*1895–15.

Height 12.7cm, length 15.24cm, width 15.24cm.

Margary Gift

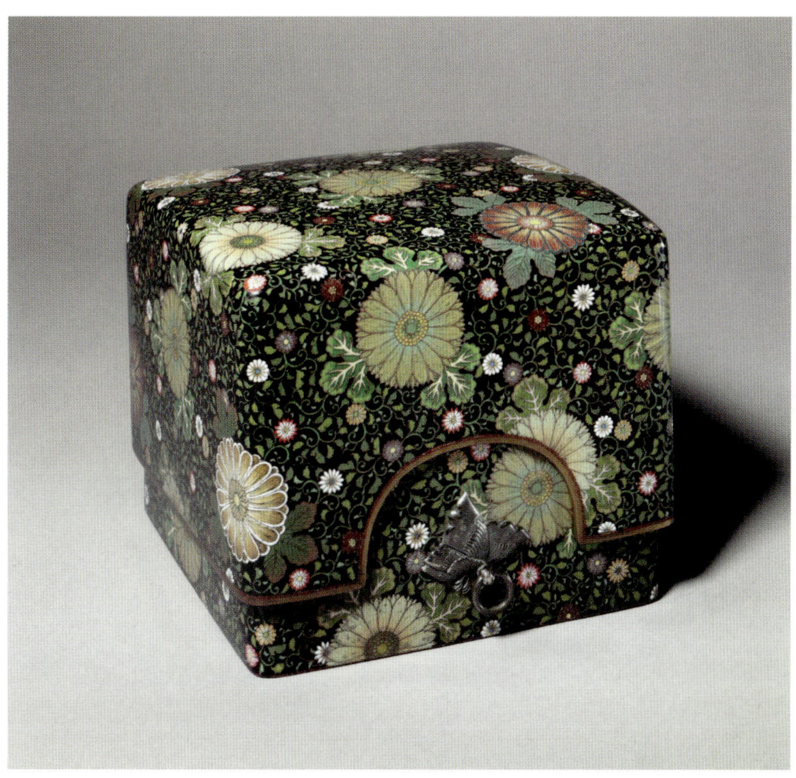

59

The table cabinet's blue enamel exterior is decorated with a spring scene of flowers, wisteria and birds; the interior, with seven drawers, of green enamel is decorated with an autumn scene of chrysanthemums, maples and exotic birds.

Unsigned, Nagoya, *c.*1905–20.

Height 19.4cm, width 12.1cm, depth 8.9cm.

Margary Gift

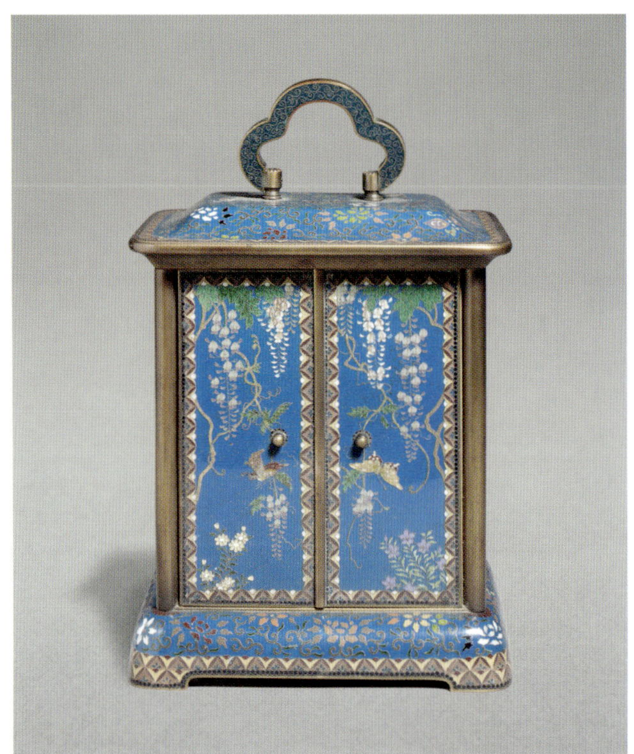

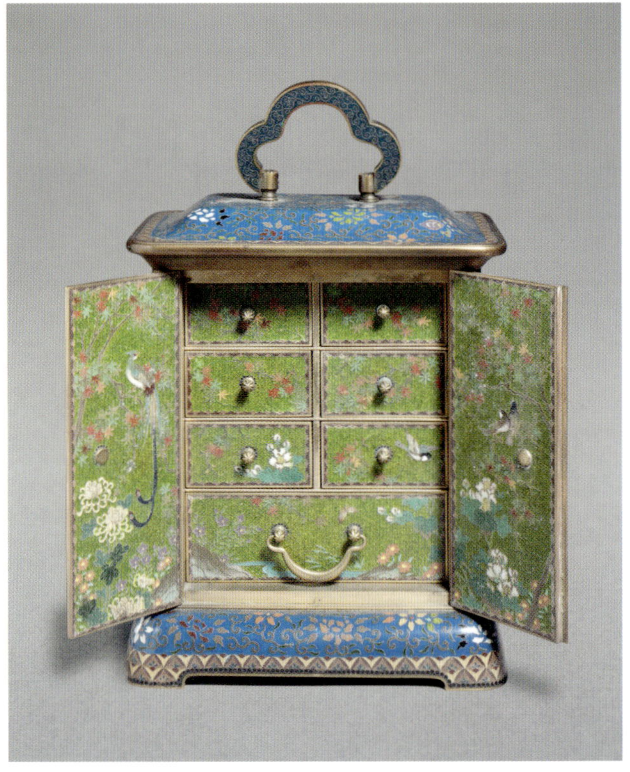

60

Vase decorated with *ho-o* (here resembling peacocks) among cloud-like *karakusa* scrolls interspersed with lotus and *hosoge* flowers.

Unsigned, possibly Ando Company, Nagoya, *c.*1912–26.

Height 13cm, width 22cm.

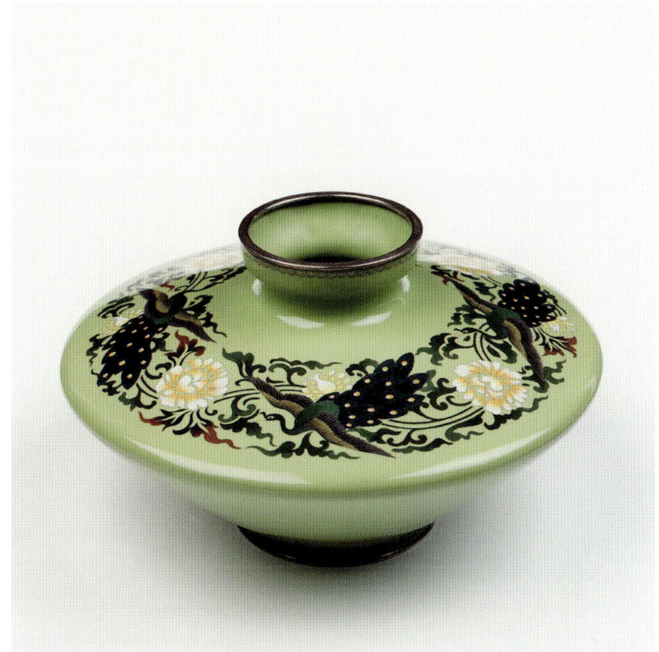

61

Chinese-shaped vase decorated in enamels with a Chinese landscape painting of a mountainous view with a temple partly hidden by a foreground of pine trees and rocks.

Mark of the Ando Company, Nagoya, *c.*1912–26.

Height 25cm, width 10cm.

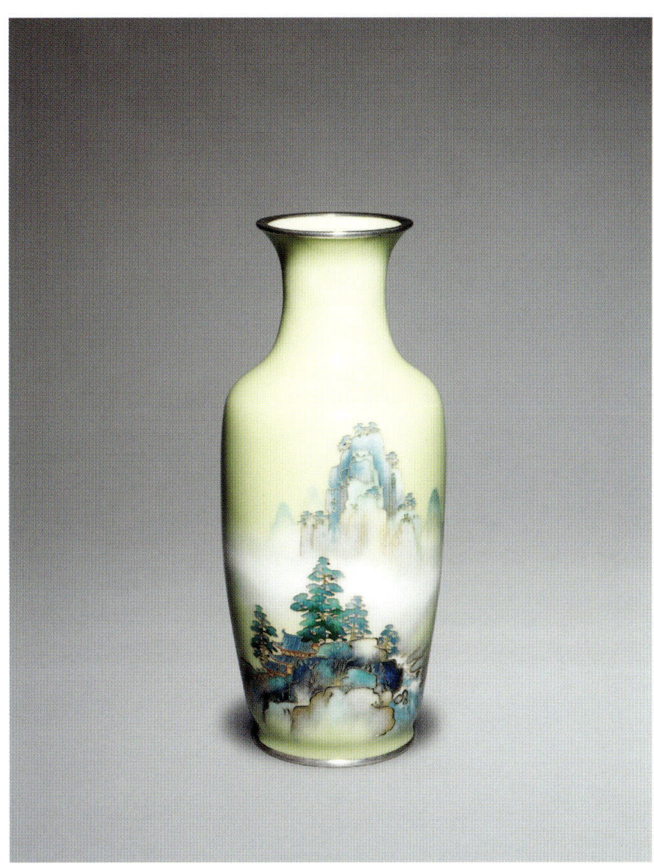

62

Pair of vases decorated with exotic birds, perched on trees with shaded green enamel leaves, exquisitely applied in a painterly manner. The birds' plumage is softly defined in subtle shades of polychrome enamels.

Mark of the Ando Company, Nagoya, *c.*1912–26.

Height 31cm, width 16cm.

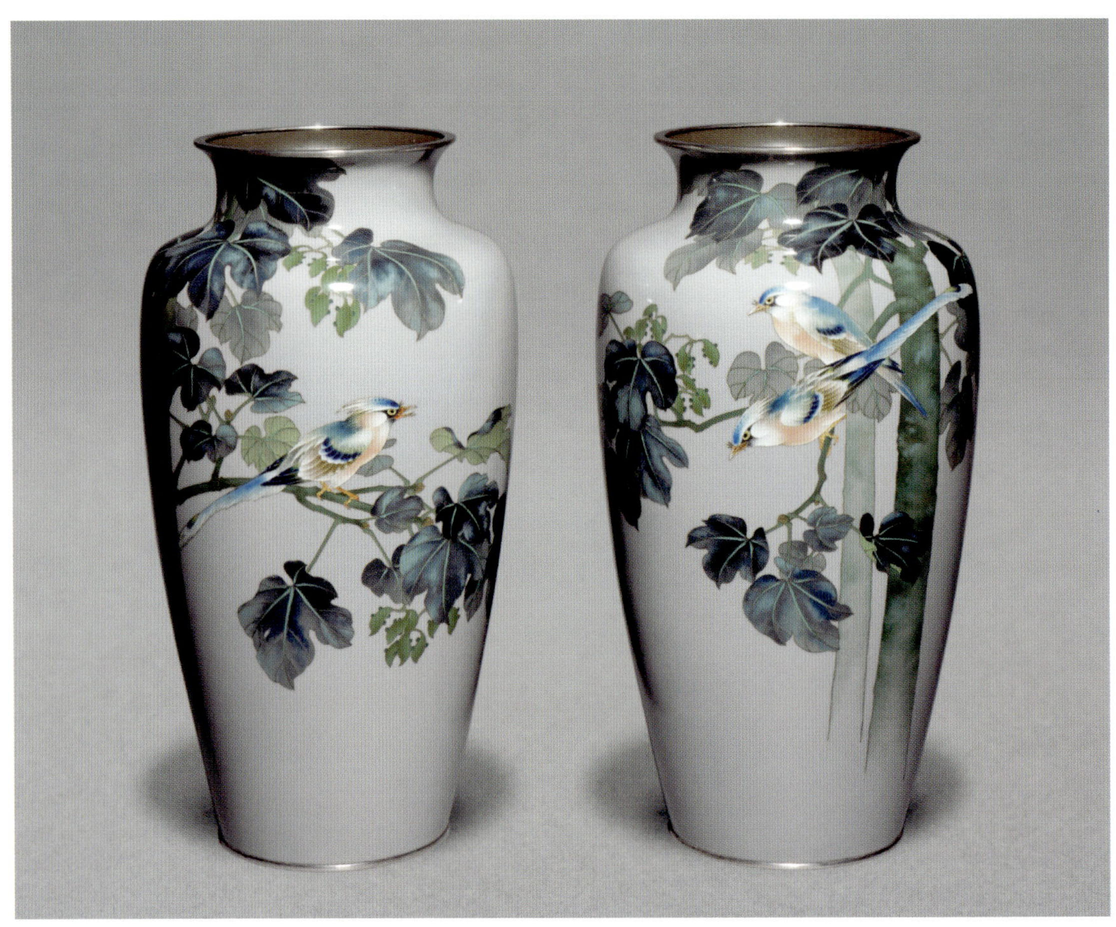

63

Two *shotai-jippo* vases
decorated with geisha at
cherry-blossom viewing
time admiring views of
the Yasaka Pagoda, one
of the most famous views
in Kyoto. These vases
would have appealed
to both Japanese and
foreign visitors to Kyoto.

Unsigned, Nagoya,
*c.*1920–40.

Height 12cm, width 8cm.

64

Vase, the shape and
decoration imitating a
Chinese bronze vessel
of the Han Dynasty
(221 BC–AD 220); details
in white *moriage* enamel.

Mark of the Ando
Company, Nagoya,
*c.*1920–50.

Height 25.5cm, width 16cm.

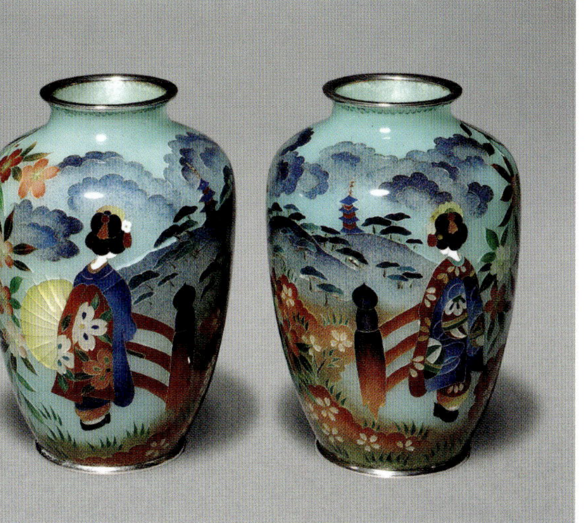

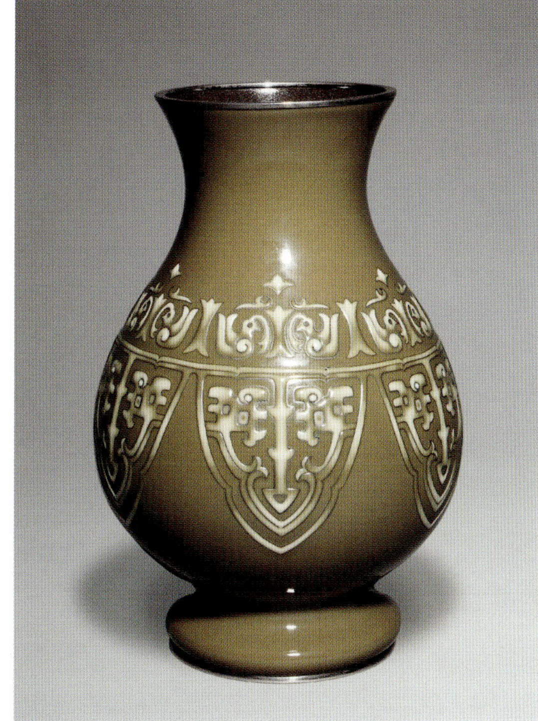

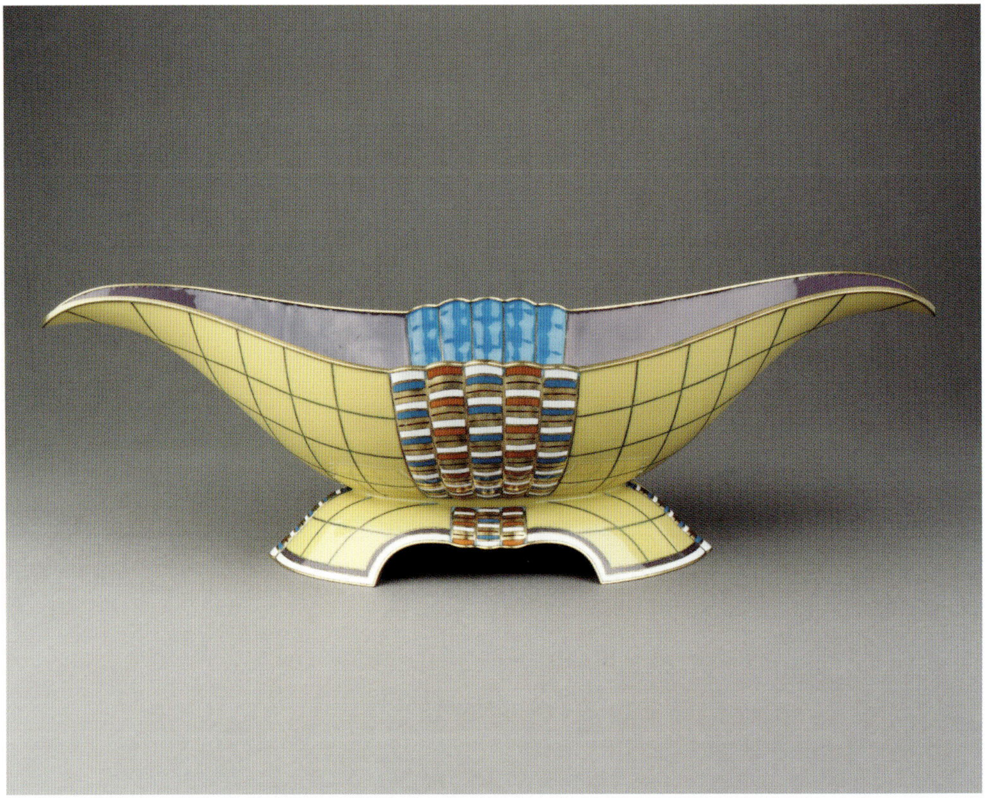

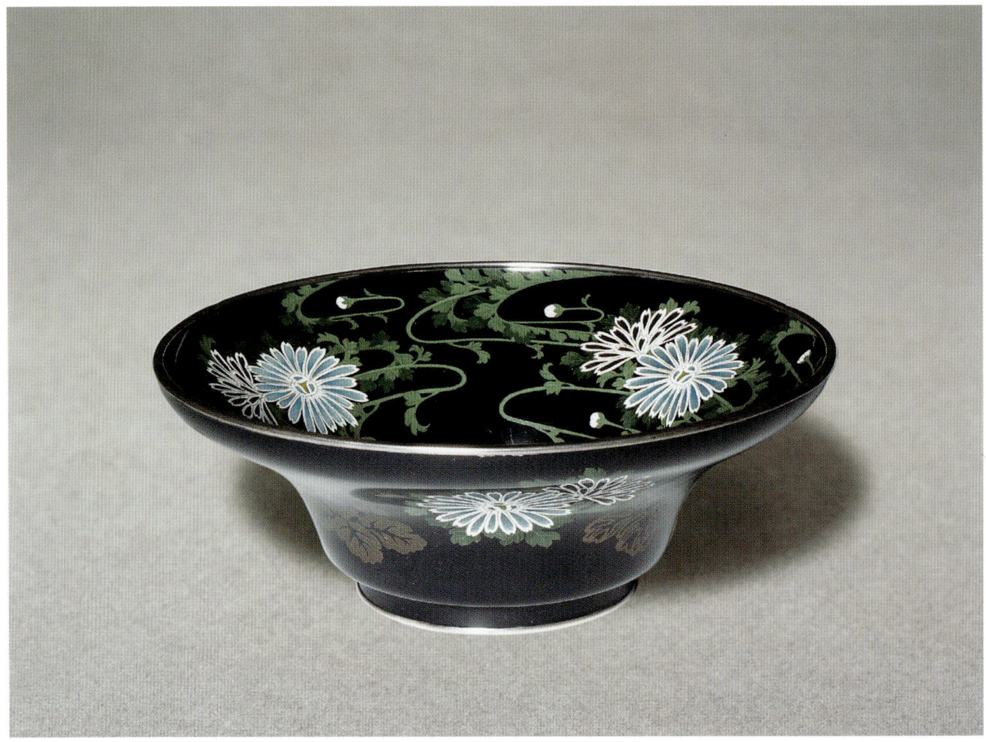

 NEW MARKETS AND CHANGING TASTES: THE PRICE OF COMMERCIAL SUCCESS

65

Fruit dish decorated
with geometrical
shapes delineated by
gilded copper wires;
the design clearly
shows the influence
of Art Deco, which
became popular in
Japan in the 1920s
and 1930s.

Mark of the Ando
Company, Nagoya,
*c.*1930–50.

Height 13cm,
width 44cm.

66

Bowl decorated
with trailing leaves
of an almost three-
dimensional quality
and chrysanthemums,
the petals of which are
executed in translucent
totai-jippo enamels in
shades of blue, purple
and white and outlined
with silver wire.

Mark of the Ando
Company, Nagoya,
*c.*1912–26.

Height 8.5cm,
diameter 23.5cm.

67

Vase with a brown
enamel ground
decorated with a
single-tree peony
blossom shaded in pink
and white on a stem
with leaves of rich
greens, all in *moriage*
enamels.

Unsigned, probably
the Ando Company,
Nagoya, *c.*1912–26.

Height 24.5cm,
width 11.5cm.

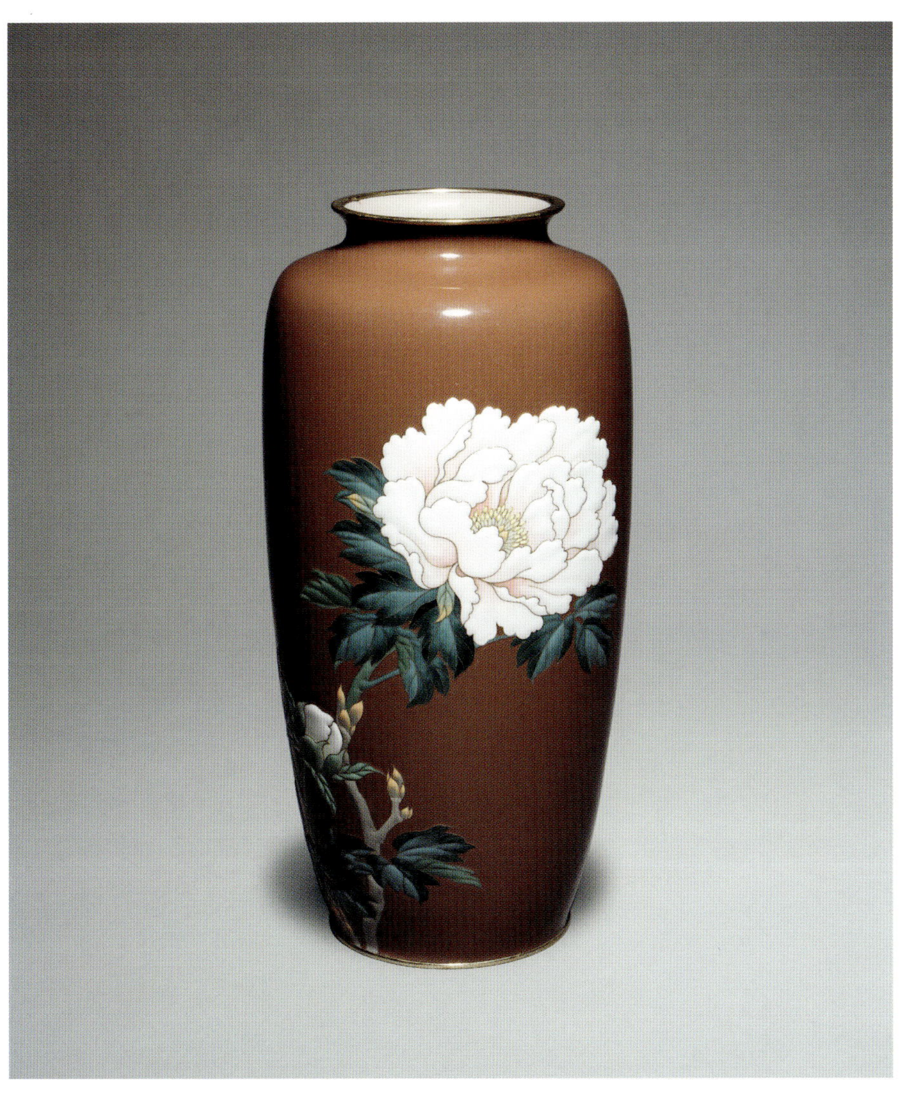

68

Vase decorated with chrysanthemums, the petals and some of their leaves are in low-relief *moriage* enamel and set against a pale pink enamel ground.

Mark of the Ando Company, Nagoya, *c*.1912–26.

Height 31cm, width 21cm.

69

Vase with superbly executed enamel decoration of bush-clover, chrysanthemums, gentians and other flowers and foliage, subtly shaded to accentuate the vibrantly naturalistic composition.

Mark of the Ando Company, Nagoya, *c*.1910–26.

Height 37.5cm, width 20cm.

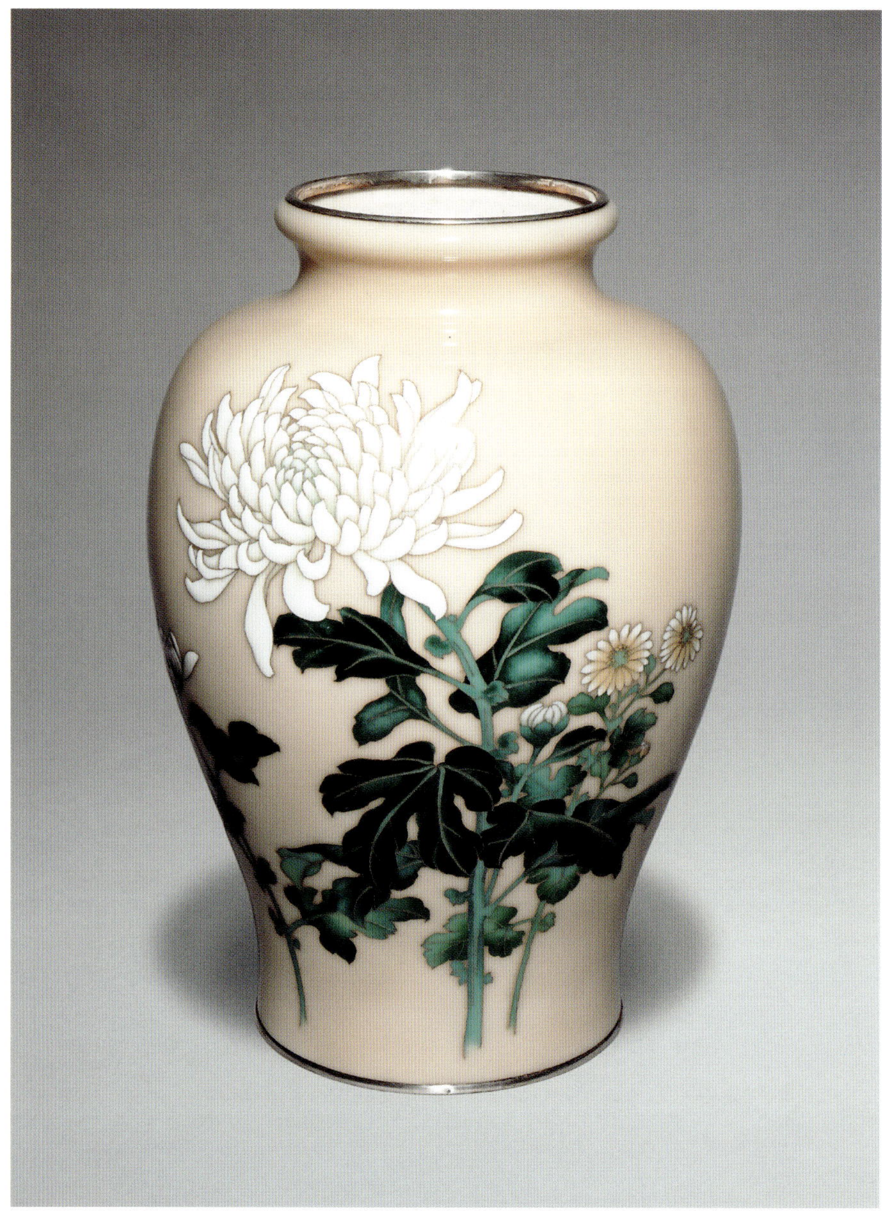

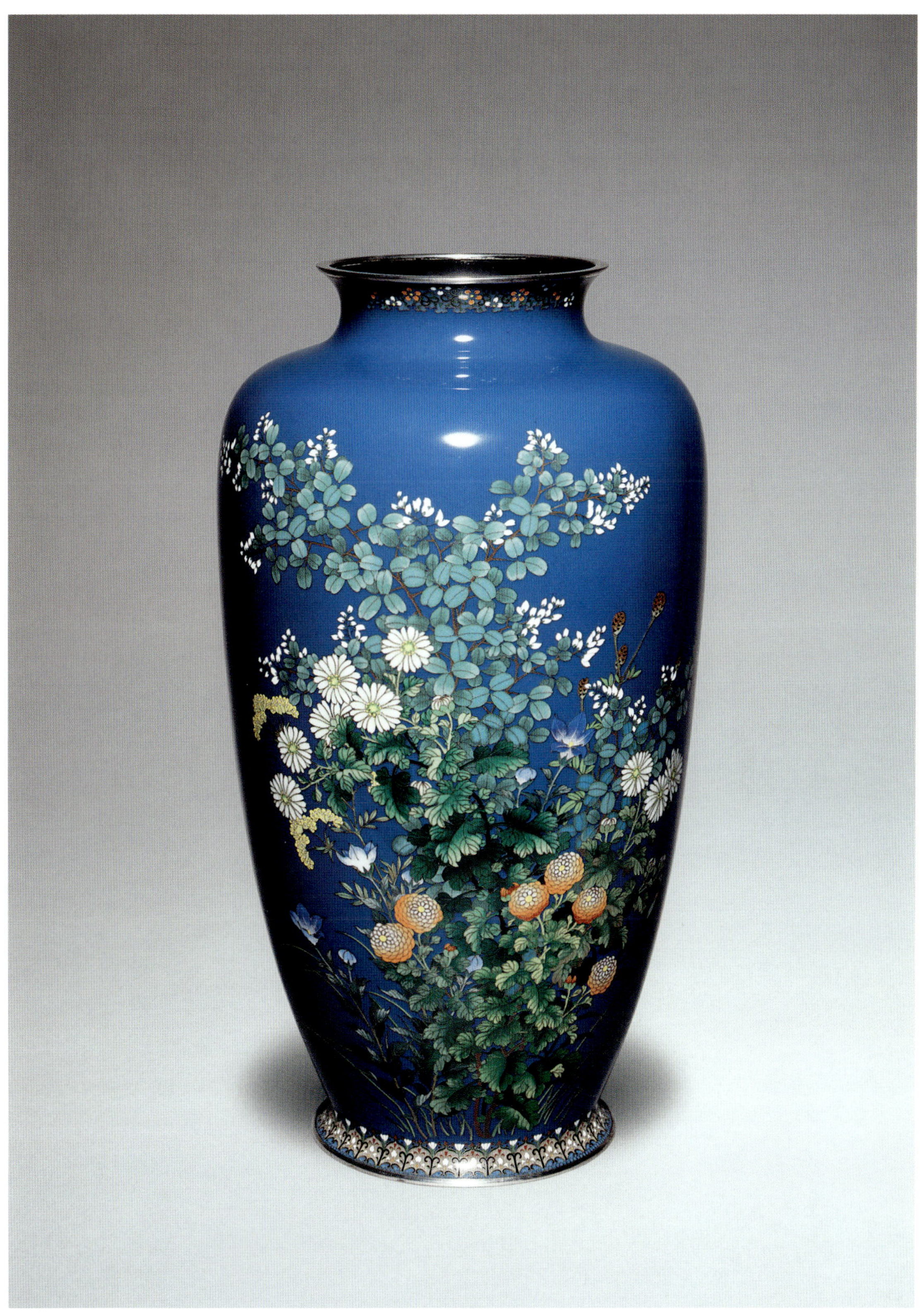

70

Vase with rich green
enamel ground decorated
with large yellow and
white shaded narcissi.

Mark of the Ando
Company, Nagoya,
c.1950–60.

Height 31cm, width 15cm.

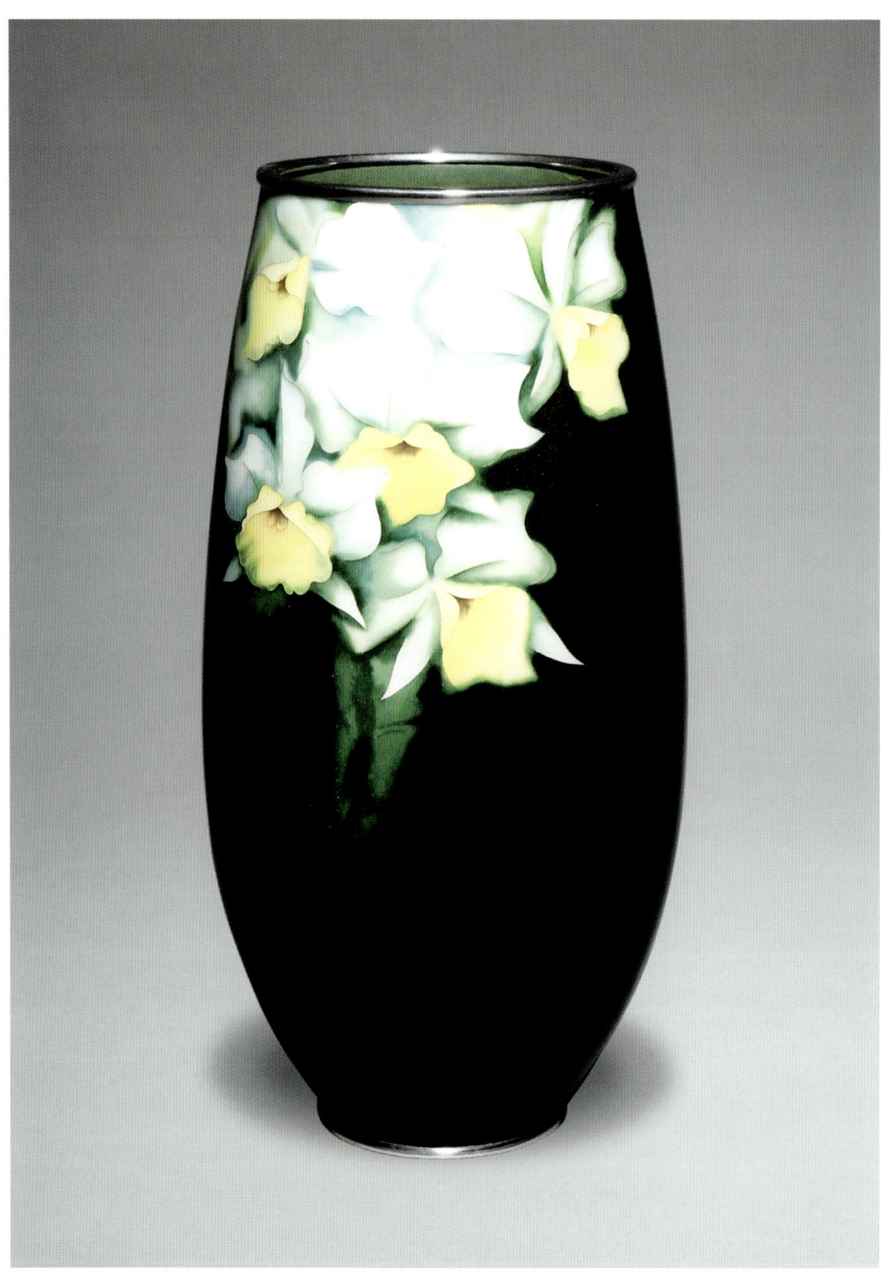

71

Vase decorated with *hosoge*, a flower associated with Buddhism which combines aspects of the peony, the lotus and other flowers.

Mark of the Ando Company, Nagoya, *c.*1930–50.

Height 23cm, width 17cm.

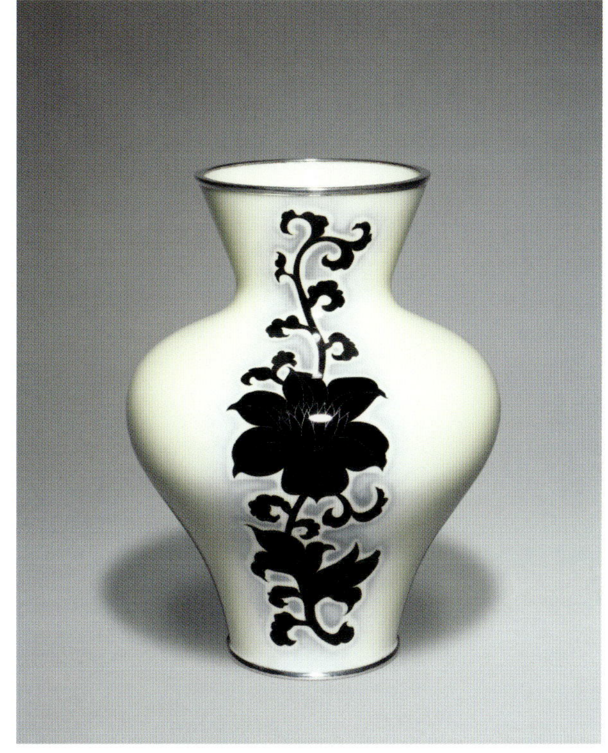

72

Pedestal vase decorated with a stylized band of dandelions in low-relief *moriage* enamel on a speckled matt dark green and brown enamel ground.

Mark of the Ando Company, Nagoya, *c.*1920–40.

Height 20cm, width 20.5cm.

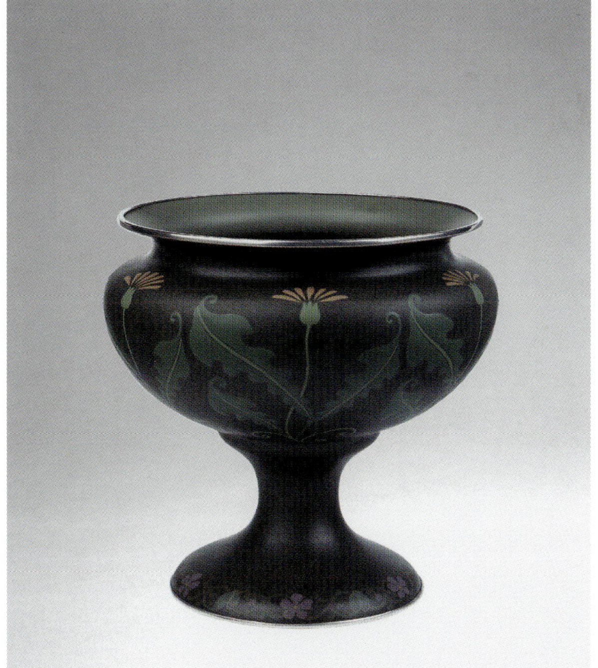

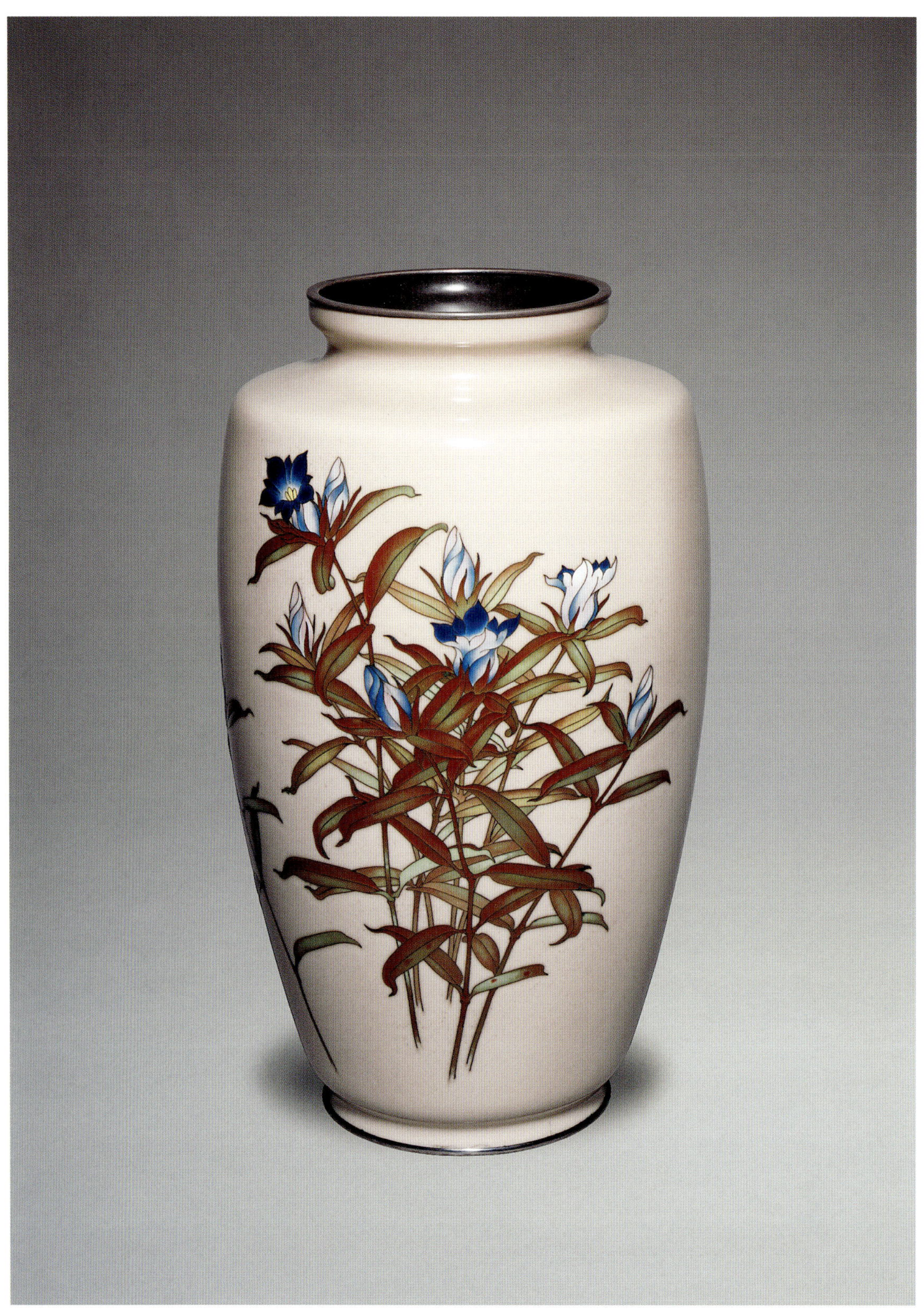

73

Vase decorated with blue and pink gentians, with some areas of the petals and leaves in low-relief *moriage* enamel on a pale beige enamel ground.

Mark of the Ando Company, Nagoya, *c.*1930–50.

Height 37cm, width 18cm.

74

Hakutai: sculptural object made from a single sheet of fluted copper enamelled with blue and silver foil circles. By Takeyama Naoki, a leading figure among a generation of young Japanese artists who have been revisiting the use of enamelling on copper.

Tokyo, 2007.

Height 32cm, width 35cm, depth 28cm.

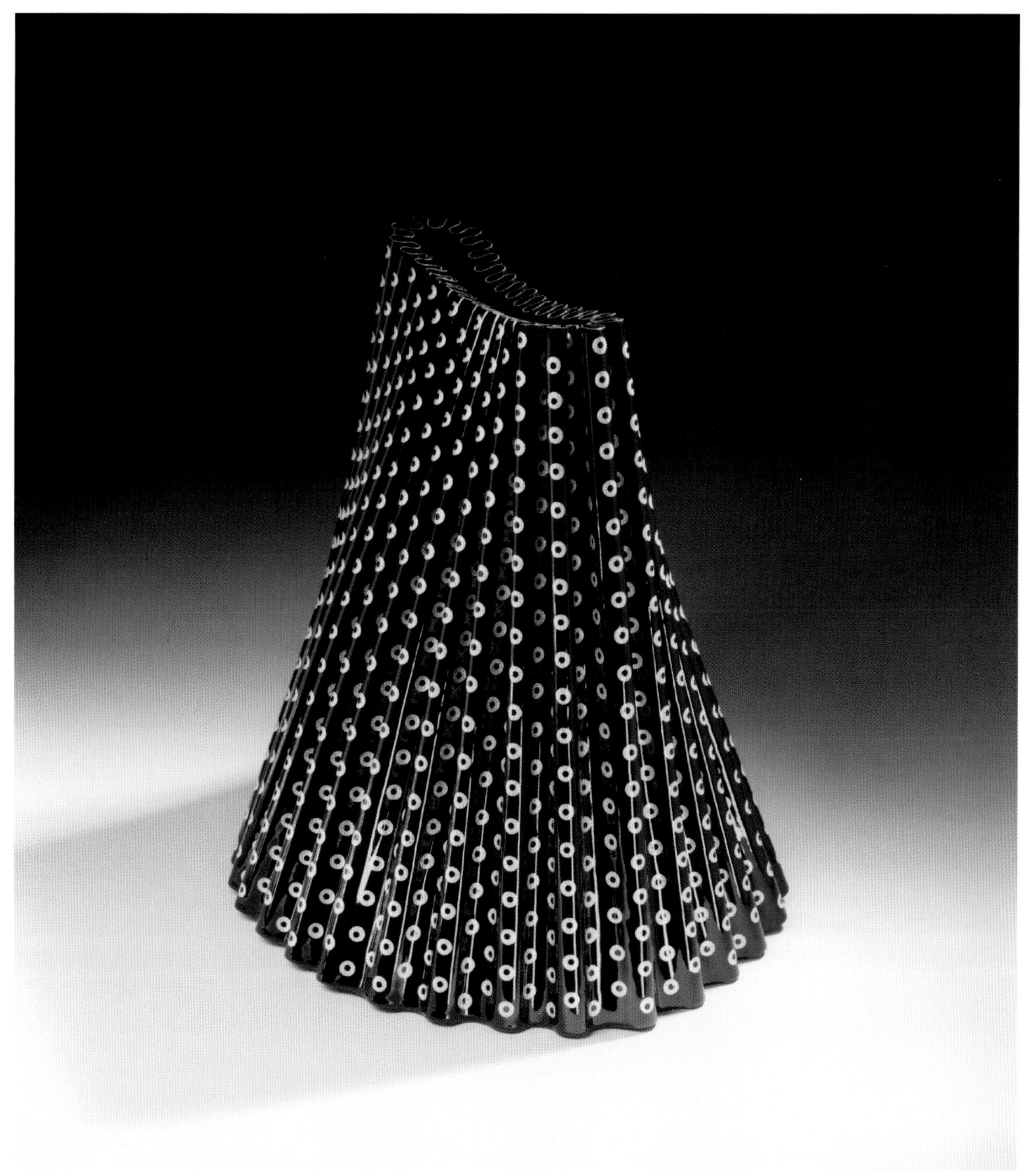

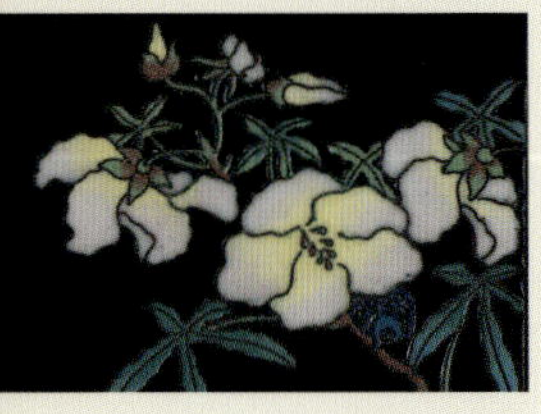

COLLECTING JAPANESE CLOISONNÉ AT THE VICTORIA AND ALBERT MUSEUM

Following the Great Exhibition of 1851, the V&A was established with the purpose of forming collections that would 'exhibit the practical application of the principles of design in the graceful arrangement of forms, and the harmonious combination of colours for the benefit of manufacturers, artisans and the general public'. The first acquisition of Japanese cloisonné enamels came from the Paris Exposition Universelle of 1867 and are the earliest documented examples of Japanese cloisonné enamels in the West. They include a 'kettle' bought for £24, and a 'sweetmeat case' for which the extraordinary sum of £60 was paid (pl.76). Both pieces are recorded as having been purchased from 'The Tycoon's Government' and were described as 'antique Japanese'.

The 'Tycoon's Government' was the Tokugawa *shogunate* in its final days of power and the vessels were either contemporary, or had been made within the previous five years, therefore representing some of the earliest examples of larger-scale, high-quality cloisonné made in Japan. Both pieces are characterized by dullish enamels on a blue ground and use considerable numbers of background wires. We do not know who made them, but they are likely to have been produced in Nagoya, possibly even by Kaji Tsunekichi.

The year 1872 saw the purchase of a dish (pl.75) for £50 from a Berlin-based dealer. When Ando Jubei visited the V&A in 1910, he pronounced that it had been made by Kaji Sataro, son of Tsunekichi. What one can say with certainty is that it could not have been more than a few years old at the time of acquisition. The next major acquisition of cloisonné enamels was from of a collection of '27 pieces of stoneware, enamels etc.' purchased in 1875 from Siegfried Bing, the Paris-based entrepreneur and dealer: 1,800 francs was paid for one unusual item which is either a brazier (*hibachi*) or an incense burner (*koro*; pl.77). In 1878 the Museum purchased for the considerable sum of £52.10 a pair of solid silver cloisonné-enamelled dishes from 'Lazenby Liberty & Co., 218 Regent Street'. Liberty's became one of the major dealers in Japanese art in London (pl.78).

In 1880, the V&A acquired several items from Christopher Dresser's company, Londos & Co. Two small unsigned vases from this group are probably, on stylistic grounds, early examples of the work of Namikawa Yasuyuki (pl.79). That they might be of Kyoto origin was first suggested by Hayashi Tadamasa (1853–1906) when he visited the V&A in 1886 to assess the Japanese collections. Hayashi had studied at what is now Tokyo University and in 1878 served as an interpreter at the Paris Exposition; he stayed on in Europe and became a significant dealer and adviser on Japanese art.

The first attributed piece of Japanese cloisonné enamel to have entered the V&A was a small dish, acquired in 1881, which Museum records state was made by Seizaburo Goto of Honcho-dori, Yokohama (pl.81). An almost identical dish was acquired at the same time, and from the same source, by the National Museum of Scotland. In 1886 the V&A received the bequest of Frank Dixon, which included several interesting examples of Nagoya enamels (pl.82) as well as two small vases which, judging from the style of wiring and colour scheme, may again be early works of Namikawa Yasuyuki (pl.83). By the 1890s the V&A was much more aware of the names of contemporary makers, though attributions continued, at times, to be a little vague or over-optimistic. Objects were confidently ascribed to Kaji Tsunekichi or Namikawa Yasuyuki (pl.26) with little in the way of fact to support the attribution.

In 1901, following the death of James Lord Bowes, the V&A acquired from the sale of his collection the bowl numbered 'Bowes Collection, Enamels No.1' (pl.84). In 1903, the Museum bought from the London dealer John Sparks its first signed piece bearing the signature of Namikawa Yasuyuki. Another object acquired from Sparks was an elegant but unsigned vase which Ando Jubei, when visiting the V&A in 1910, informed us that he had made (pl.85).

Ando's visit to the V&A took place at the time of the Japan-British Exhibition at White City, London, where his company had a stand. Correspondence in Museum archives record how the V&A rejected an offer from Ando of ten contemporary works including a vase with a 'wireless design of Mount Fuji' and several vases of 'raised enamel'. The Museum authorities justified their decision in straightforward terms: 'The board do not desire to purchase for this Museum the specimens of modern enamelling' (V&A Nominal File, J. Ando). This unfortunate missed opportunity to purchase works by Ando Jubei can be explained by the fact that, by the beginning of the twentieth century, the V&A had adopted a policy of acquiring mostly historical works of art and had more or less stopped buying anything new. However, the recent gift of a substantial number

of fine works by Ando from the collection of Mr Edwin Davies
has ensured that this omission has now been rectified.

The V&A was not yet immune from the 'taxonomic obsession' of earlier years, and the period 1910–31 saw the acquisition of huge numbers of sword fittings (notably the Hildburgh
gift of 1931), which included fine examples of inlaid enamels
(pl.86). In 1925, not a time when Japanese art had a particularly
high profile, the V&A, perhaps harking back to its original
aims of inspiring designers, commissioned a set of examples of
cloisonné-manufacture processes from Shozo Kato (pl.87). It is
unclear if this is the same Kato who was also a well-established
dealer based in London. In 1969 a small collection, including
several works by Namikawa Yasuyuki, was bequeathed to the
V&A (pl.88). The V&A's cloisonné collection had otherwise
hardly grown since Ando's visit, but the very recent acquisition
of an elegant lidded container (pl.89) was a positive move to
expand the V&A collections.

Thanks now to the benefaction of Mr Edwin Davies and
his generous gift, the V&A will be now able to research and
expand its collection of cloisonné enamels, thereby giving due
recognition to an aspect of Japan's artistic legacy that has been
the focus of increasing interest among museums and collectors during the last fifteen years. In addition, we will be able to
work more with national and international collections thereby
enabling a wider audience to become aware of and appreciate
this superb art form.

It was, and is still, in the West where many of the best collections of Japanese cloisonné enamels are to be found and
from where the impetus to acknowledge the artistry and skills
of the enamel craftsman has mostly come. The forming, exhib-
iting and publishing of these superb collections have enabled
scholars, curators, collectors and the wider public in both the
West and in Japan itself to re-evaluate Japanese cloisonné and
other arts of the Meiji period. Recently in Japan, there have
been several important and popular exhibitions that have
focused on this period and which have, significantly, increased
awareness of the importance of Japan's contribution to the arts,
especially at the great world expositions of the nineteenth and
early twentieth centuries.

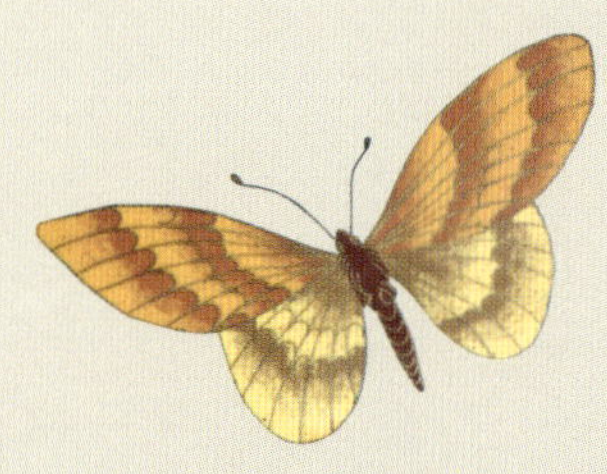

Dish decorated in brass wires on a ground of stylized floral and geometrical motifs with two dragons fighting for the sacred Buddhist pearl of wisdom.

Unsigned – in 1910, Ando Jubei stated that this dish was made by Kaji Sataro, son of Tsunekichi – Nagoya, c.1865–70.

Diameter 54.1cm.

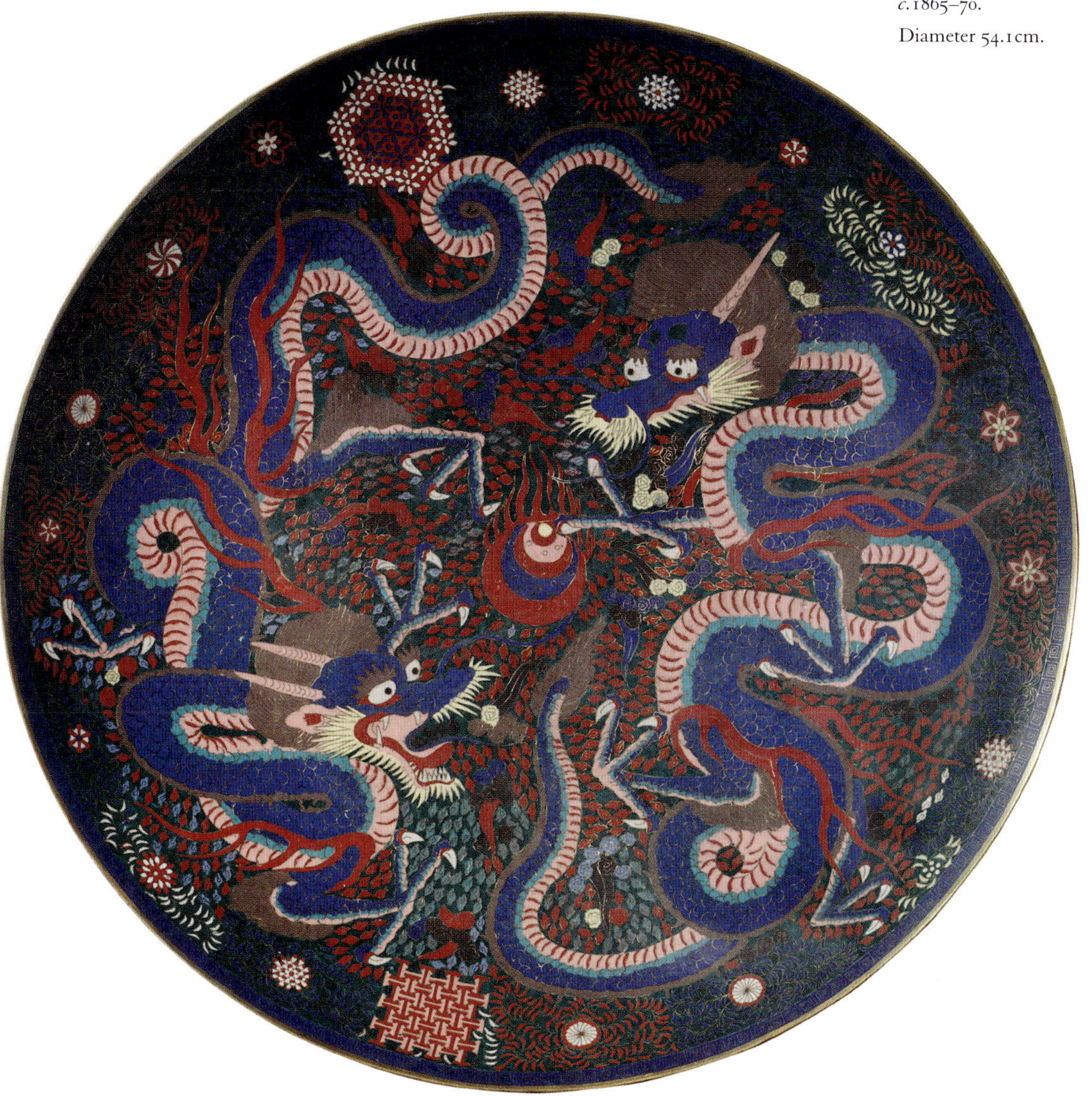

76

Tiered sweetmeat case
(*jubako*) decorated
with floral and abstract
motifs. The lid has a
scene of cranes and
pines on the legendary
mountain-island Horai,
a place of eternal youth
and immortality.

Unsigned, Nagoya,
c.1860.

Height 19.7cm.

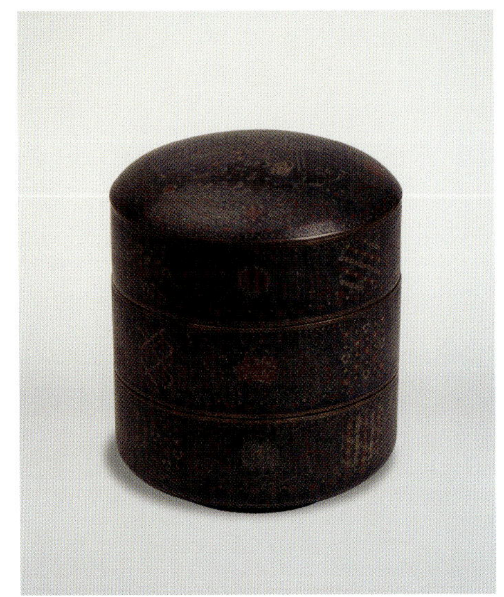

77

Incense burner (*koro*)
or brazier (*hibachi*)
decorated with scrolling
karakusa, cloud and bat
motifs and a type of *ho-o*,
all in twisted silver wire
on a pale blue enamel
ground.

Unsigned, Nagoya,
c.1865–70.

Overall height 27.9cm.

Purchased from
Siegfried Bing.

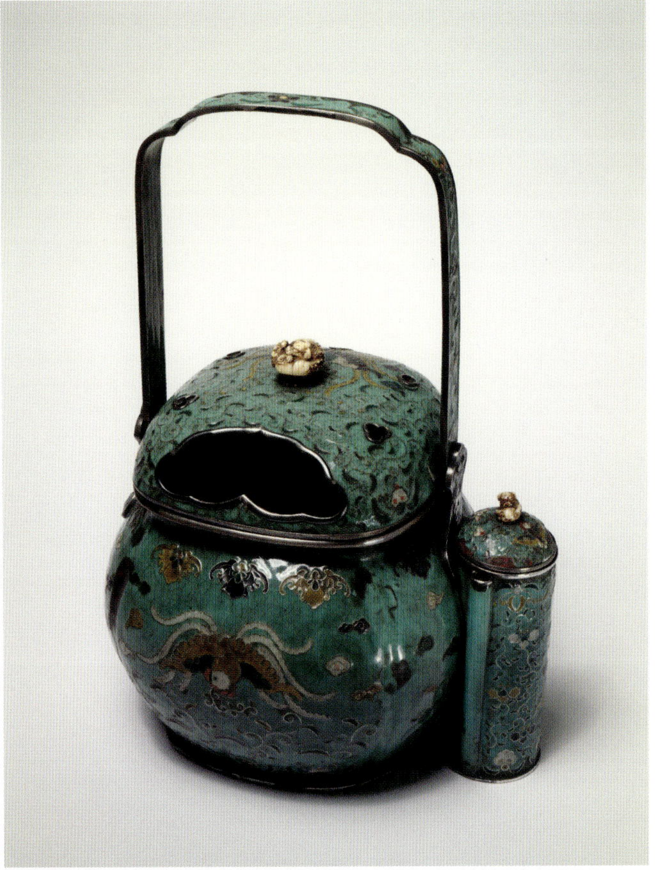

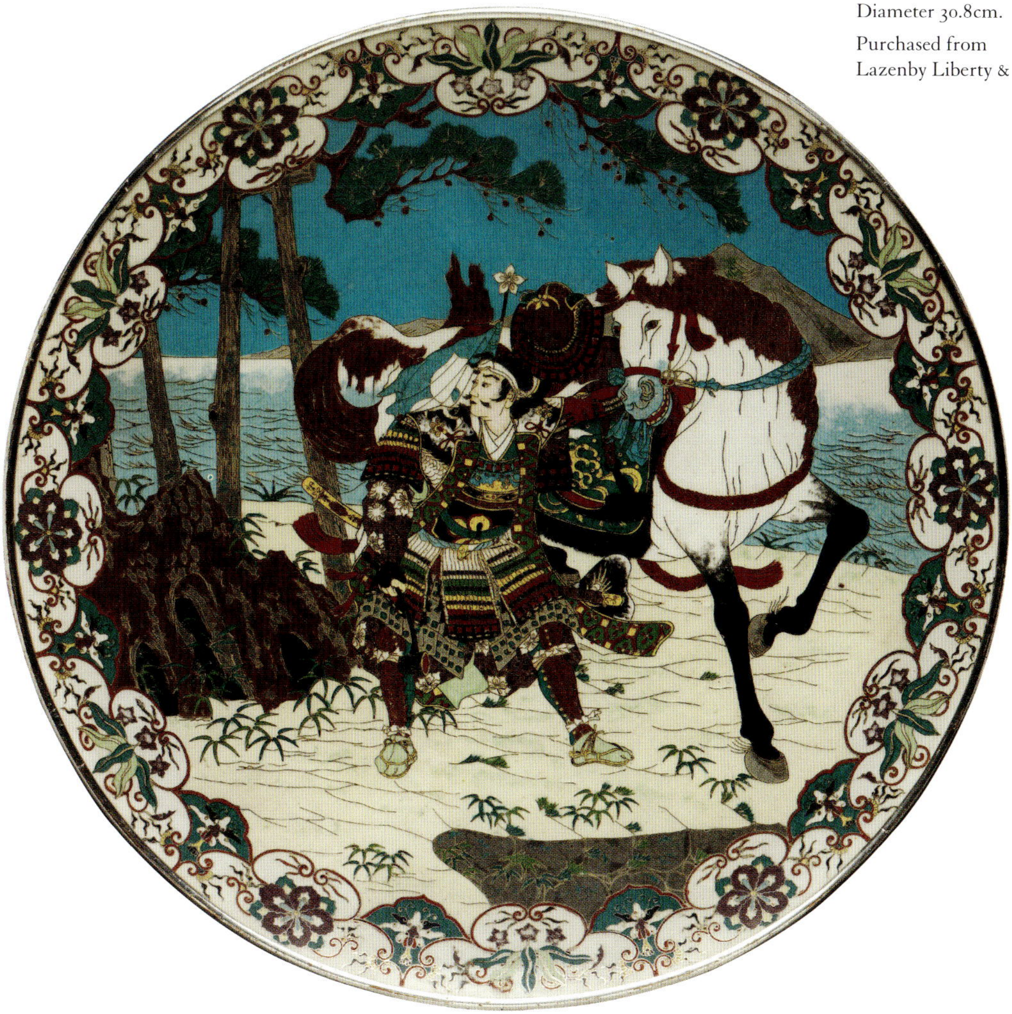

78

Silver dish (one of a pair) with stylized floral borders and a central scene of a samurai, possibly one from the twelfth-century 'war tales', which idealized the samurai and were popular during the Meiji period.

Unsigned, Nagoya, *c.*1870–75.

Diameter 30.8cm.

Purchased from Lazenby Liberty & Co.

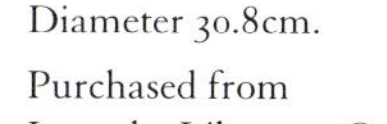

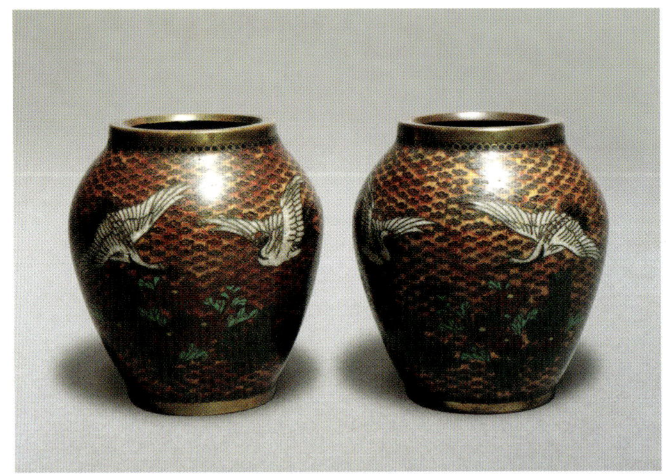

79

Pair of vases decorated with stylized clouds, Japanese cranes, chrysanthemums and pine-boughs.

Unsigned, but attributed to Namikawa Yasuyuki, Kyoto, *c.*1870–80.

Height 8.6cm.

Purchased from Londos & Co.

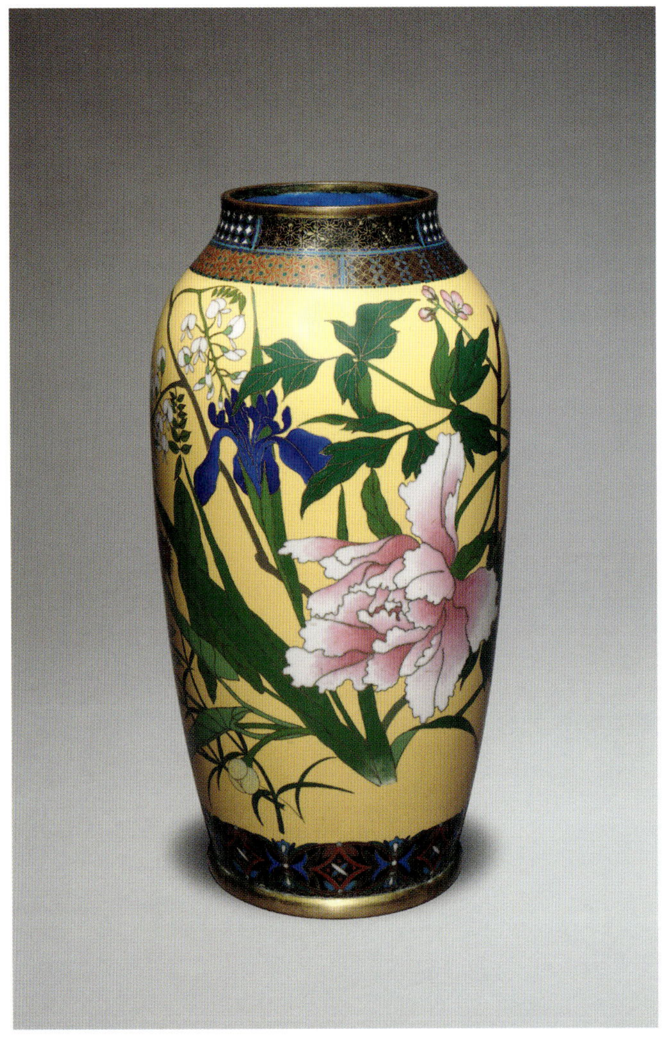

80

Vase with decoration of flowers including an iris and a peony on a yellow enamel ground. This type of enamelware influenced those produced by Elkington & Co., the Birmingham-based manufacturers of around the same period.

Unsigned, Nagoya, *c.*1875–80.

Height 25.4cm, diameter 13cm.

Purchased from Londos & Co.

Dish decorated with
a panel showing a
seated samurai in full
armour surrounded
by geometric diaper
patterns; the back
is decorated with
butterflies and
stylized flowers.

Unsigned but
attributed to
Seizaburo Goto
of Honcho-dori,
Yokohama, *c.*1875–80.

Diameter 30.5cm.

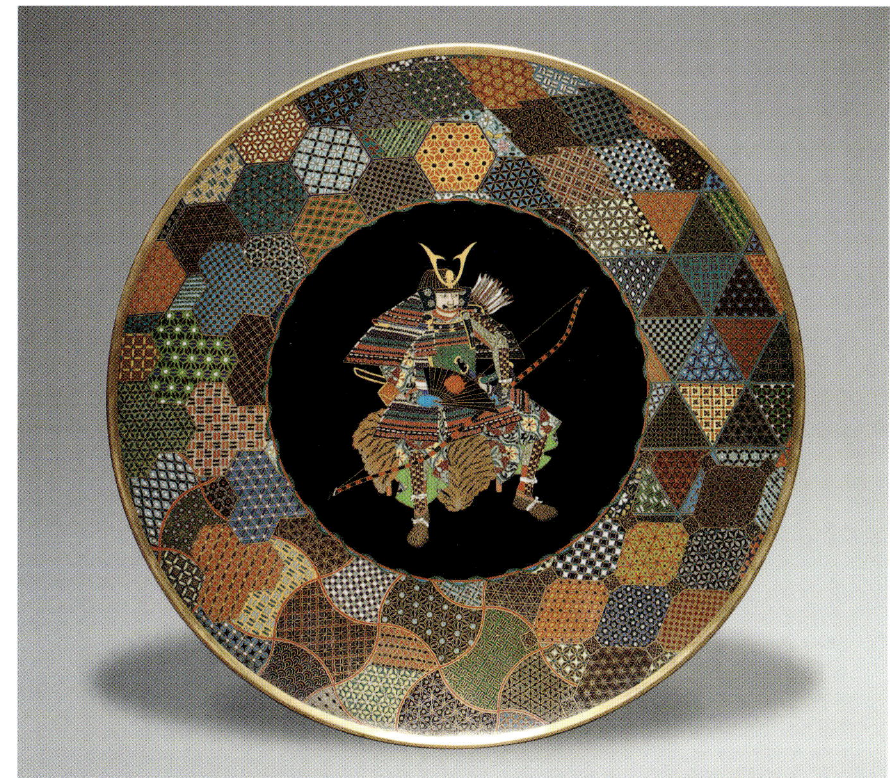

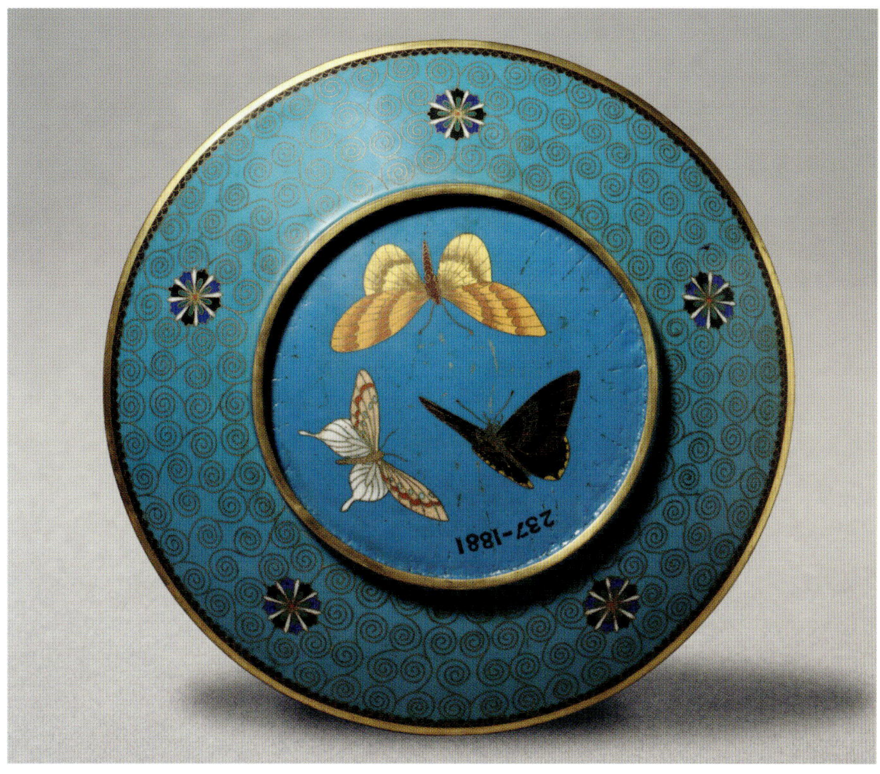

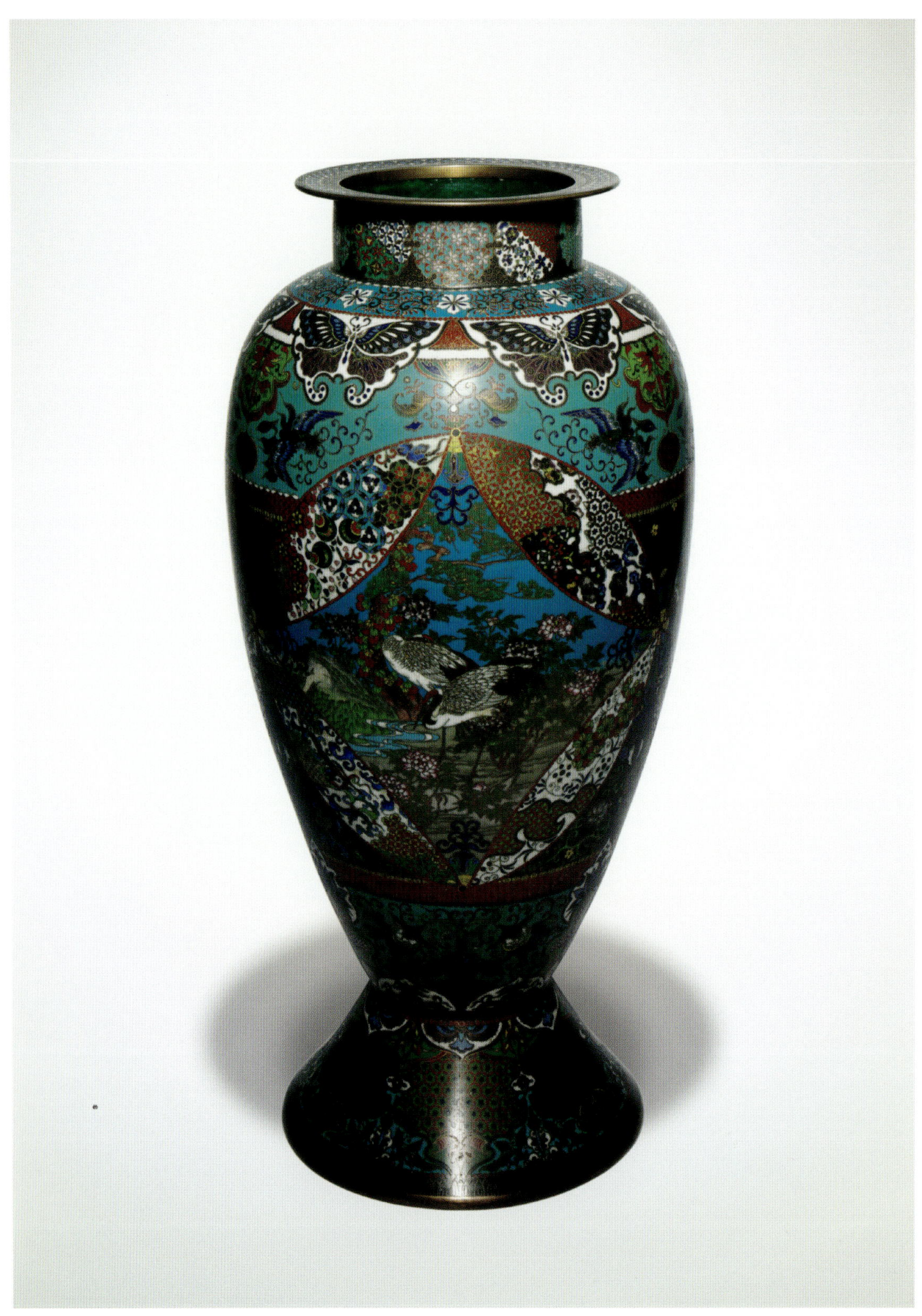

82

Vase decorated with
a *shippo*-shaped
panel of two cranes,
abstract geometric
and floral patterns,
large butterflies and
mythical birds.

Unsigned, Nagoya,
*c.*1870–80.

Height 55.3cm.

Dixon Bequest

83

Pair of vases
decorated with
butterflies and stylized
chrysanthemums.

Unsigned but attributed
to Namikawa Yasuyuki,
Kyoto, *c.*1870–80.

Height 8.6cm.

Dixon Bequest

84

Bowl decorated with
four Chinese philosophers
(one visible) on the
exterior with a dragon
in the interior, all on a
ground of stylized clouds
and abstract floral motifs.

Unsigned, Nagoya,
*c.*1865–70.

Height 8.8cm,
diameter 19.1cm.

Purchased from the sale
of the Bowes collection

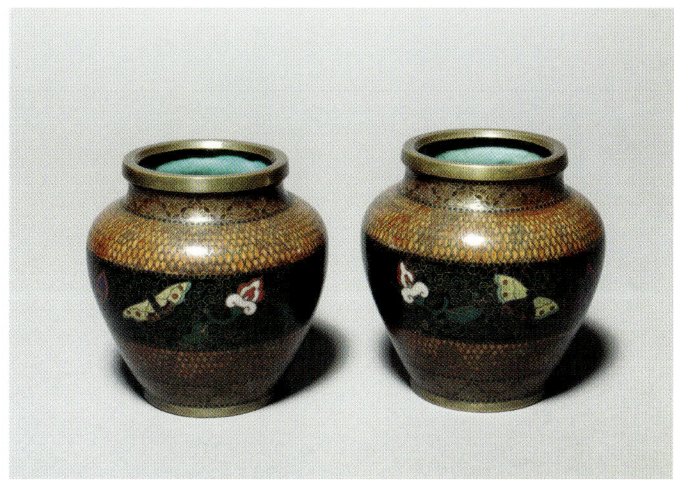

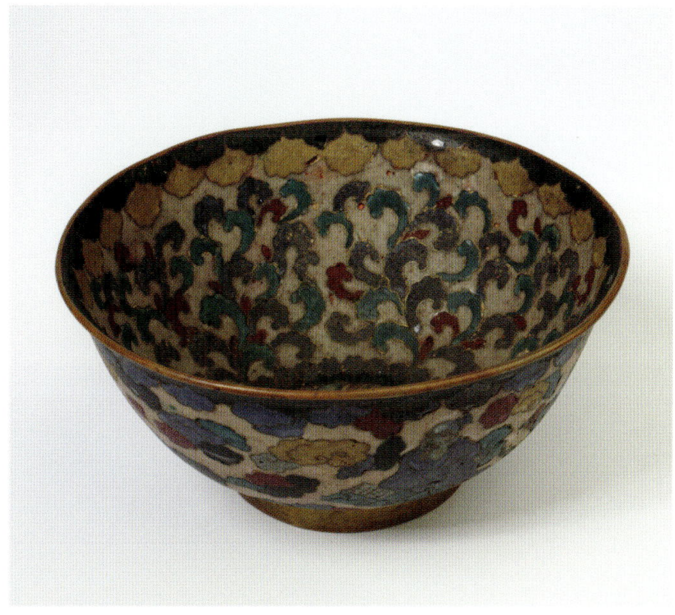

85

Vase with silver-wire
decoration of wisteria
emerging from stylized
clouds.

Unsigned but attributed
to Ando Jubei, Nagoya,
c.1895–1900.

Height 30.8cm.

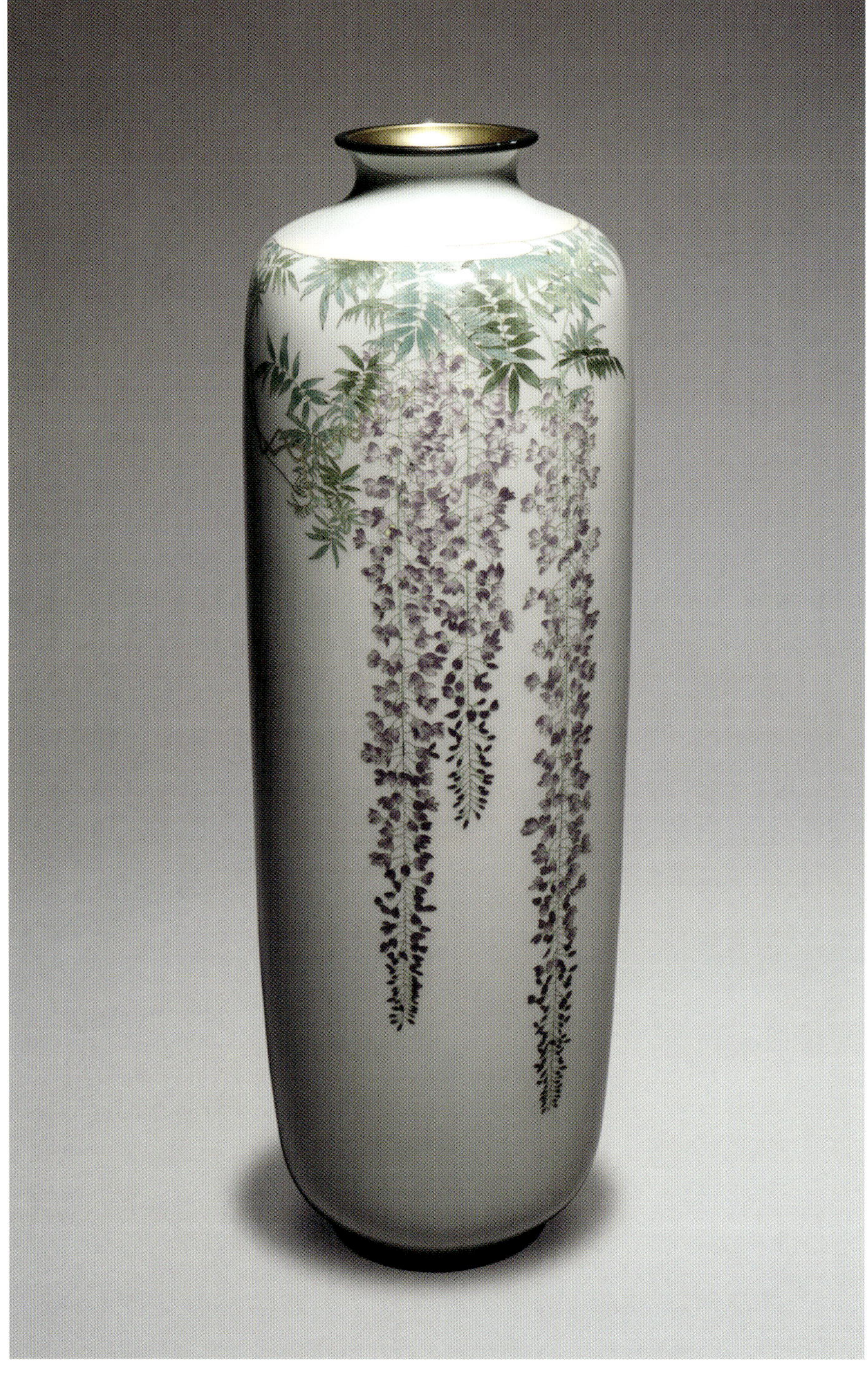

86

Two sword guards
(*tsuba*) and knife
handle (*kozuka*).

Unsigned, *c.*1700–1800.

Height (left *tsuba*)
5.7cm, width 4.7cm;
height (right *tsuba*)
5.6cm, width 4.7cm;
length (*kozuka*) 9.8cm.

(left *tsuba*) Gift of
Sir Arthur H. Church

(right *tsuba*) Gift of
W.L. Hildburgh

(*kozuka*) Gift of the
Misses Alexander

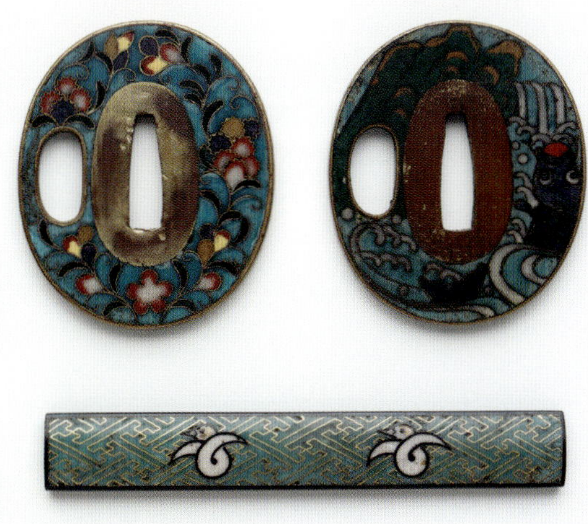

87

Samples showing
cloisonné-
enamel processes,
commissioned by the
V&A from Shozo
Kato of Birmingham.

Height (drawing)
9.2cm, width 8.5cm;
height (plates) 8.9cm,
width 8.3cm.

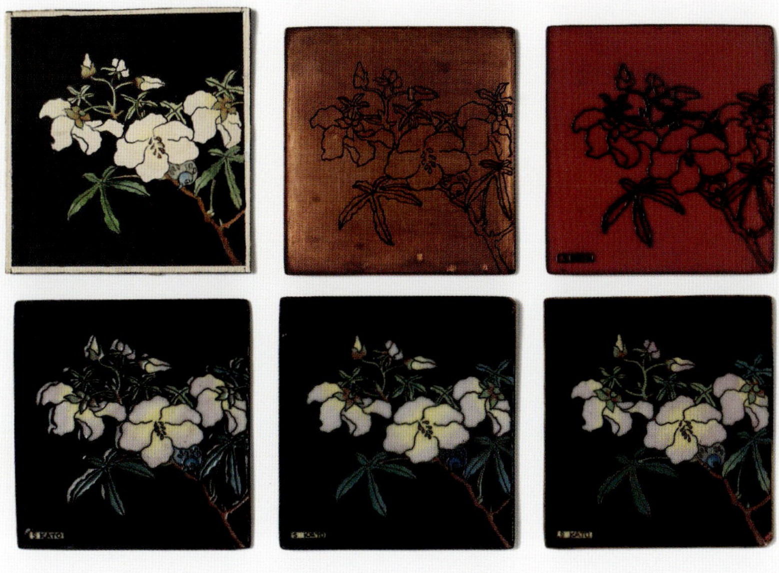

88

Lidded vase with
lilies and a sparrow
in flight, all in silver
wire on a mirror-black
enamel ground.

Mark 'Kyoto
Namikawa
[Yasuyuki]', Kyoto,
c.1890–1910.

Height 10.1cm,
diameter 8.1cm.

Margary Gift

89

Lidded bowl with
decoration of two
rabbits among flowers
within a border of
karakusa and *shippo*
motifs.

Unsigned, but possibly
by Nagoya Shippo
Kaisha, Nagoya,
c.1875–80.

Diameter 24.8cm.

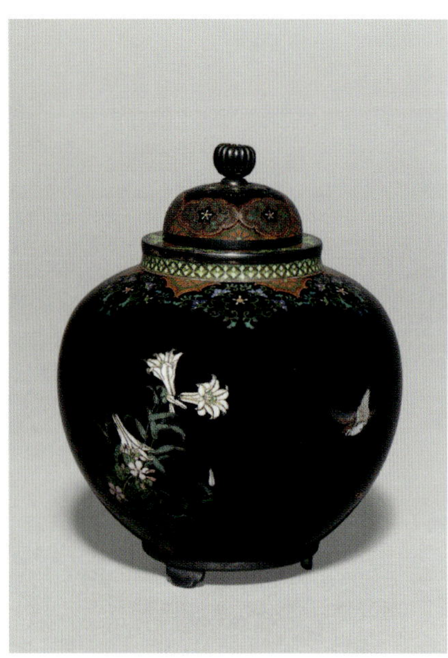

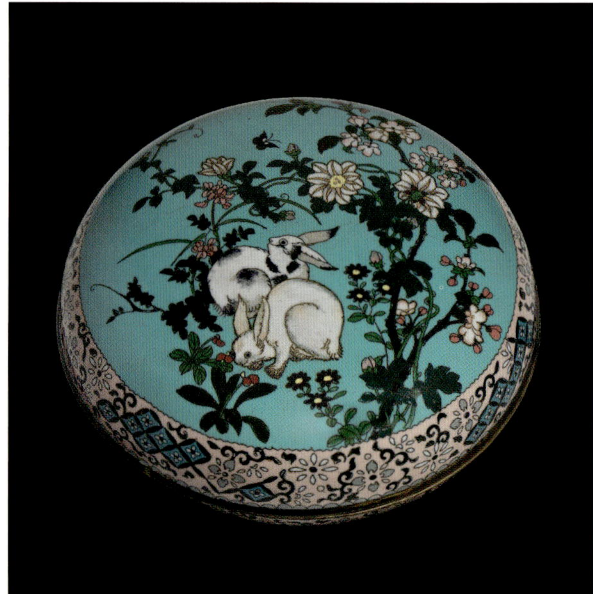

GLOSSARY

Akasuke: a transparent red enamel sometimes called 'pigeon's-blood'.

Chakinseki: 'tea-dust' effect created by including a sprinkling of gold or brass dust in the enamel.

Ginbari: the technique of laying silver foil on an object before applying a coat of clear enamel.

Ho-o: a mythical and auspicious phoenix-like bird originally found in Chinese art and associated with Buddhism.

Hosoge: a mythical flower associated with Buddhism, which combines aspects of the peony, the lotus and other flowers.

Jungin: 'pure silver', a mark found stamped on the base-plates of some cloisonné vessels.

Karakusa: 'Chinese grasses', a scrolling motif frequently found on cloisonné enamels.

Kirin: a mythical hooved and horned creature associated with prosperity. The name has long been associated with the giraffe – which is known by the name '*kirin*' in Japan today.

Moriage: 'piled-up', the technique of applying enamels in layers so that they are in relief to the body of the vessel.

Musen: 'without wires', the enamelling technique where the wires are either completely hidden or are removed before the firing to create a softly outlined decoration.

Nanako: 'fish-roe' effect produced by hammering a metal body to produce a regular pattern of small dots on the surface.

Sakigake: 'pioneer', the seal used by Namikawa Sosuke from *c.*1893

Shakudo: an alloy of copper with a small percentage of gold that is patinated to a blue-black colour.

Shippo motif: a geometric pattern based on four spindles arranged within in a circle with ends touching, and sometimes enclosing floral motifs, diamonds or stars.

Shinchu: a brass-like alloy of copper and zinc.

Shosen: literally 'few' or 'limited' wires, the technique where the number of wires was kept to a minimum and used only to delineate details of a design.

Shotai-jippo: 'eliminated body enamel', whereby the metal body of a vessel is dissolved after firing and polishing to create a stained-glass finish.

Tomei-jippo: transparent or translucent enamel through which areas of the base metal, often chased, can be seen.

Totai-jippo: pierced body enamel, the technique where a design is cut into the body of a vessel prior to enamelling.

Tsuiki-jippo: the technique where a design is hammered into the body and then covered in foil prior to enamelling and often used with '*ginbari*'

Yusen: 'with wires', the standard technique of creating cloisonné designs enclosed within wires.

Zogan: (*champlevé*) enamels inlaid into a hollow in the body of a vessel.

SELECT BIBLIOGRAPHY

Alcock, Sir Rutherford, *Art and Art Industries in Japan* (London, 1878)

Blair, Dorothy, 'The Cloisonné-backed Mirror in the Shosoin' in *The Journal of Glass Studies*, Vol.II (New York, 1960)

Bowes, James L., *Japanese Enamels, with Illustrations from the Examples in the Bowes Collection* (Liverpool, 1884)

Bowes, James L., *Notes on Shippo* (London, 1895)

Brinkley, Captain F., *Japan, its History, Arts and Literature: Pictorial and Applied Art*, Vol.VII, *Keramic Art*, Vol.VIII (Boston and Tokyo: Tokyo edition [limited edition number 199], 1901)

Coben, Lawrence A. and Dorothy C. Ferster, *Japanese Cloisonné: History, Technique and Appreciation* (New York and Tokyo, 1982)

Earle, Joe and Gregory Irvine (eds.), *Japanese Art and Design, The Toshiba Gallery at the Victoria and Albert Museum* (London, 2009)

Earle, Joe, *Splendors of Meiji, Treasures of Imperial Japan* (St Petersburg, Florida, 1999)

Harada, Jiro, 'Japanese Art and Artists of Today – VI. Cloisonné Enamels' in *The Studio*, June 1911

Harris, Victor, *Japanese Imperial Craftsmen: Meiji Art from the Khalili Collection* (London, 1994)

Impey, Oliver and Malcolm Fairley, *The Dragon King of the Sea* (Oxford, 1991)

Irvine, Gregory, *Japanese Cloisonné* (London, 2006)

Irvine, Gregory, 'Shippoyaki: the Japanese Art of Enamelling,' pp.76–86 in *Arts of Asia*, Vol.33, No.5, September–October 2005

Meiji no Takara, *Treasures of Imperial Japan, The Nasser D. Khalili Collection of Japanese Art*, Vol.III, *Enamel* (London, 1994)

Mintz, Robert, *Japanese Cloisonné Enamels: the Stephen W. Fisher Collection* (Baltimore, 2010)

Nakahara, Tessen, *Kyo Shippo Monyo-shu* (Kyoto, 1991)

Ponting, Herbert, *In Lotus Land Japan* (London, 1910)

Schneider, Frederic T., *The Art of Cloisonné Enamels: History, Techniques, Artists, 1600 to the Present* (Jefferson, California, 2010)

Suzuki, Norio, *Nihon no Shippo* (Kyoto, 1979)

The Modern Era of Shippo, Japanese Cloisonné, exhibition catalogue, Museum of the Imperial Collections, Sannomaru Shozokan (Tokyo, 2004)

Yoshino, Gary H., *Japanese Cloisonné Enamels: a Private Collector's Notes and Reference Guide* (Orange County, California, 2007)

LIST OF OBJECTS

SIGNATURES

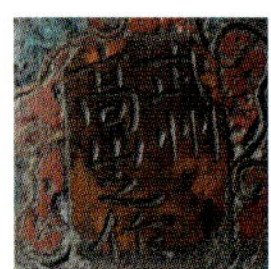

Plate. 12
V&A: M.546–1911

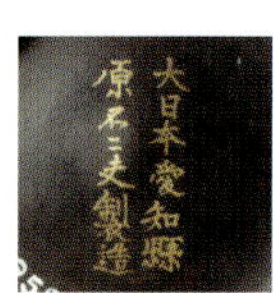

Plate. 18
V&A: M.21–1958

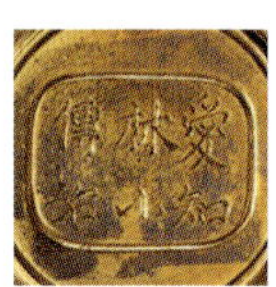

Plate. 19
V&A: FE.21:1–2011

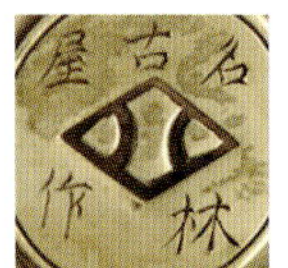

Plate. 20
V&A: FE.28:1–2011

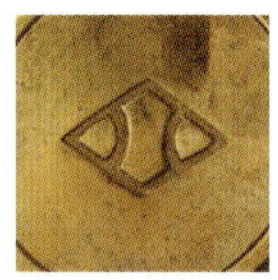

Plate. 21
V&A: FE.34:1–2011

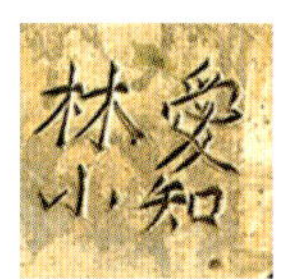

Plate. 22
V&A: FE. 40:1–2011

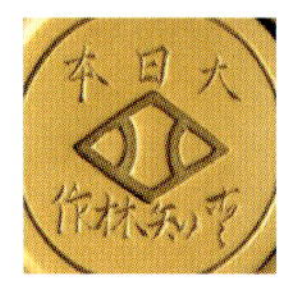

Plate. 24
V&A: FE. 55:1–2011
V&A: FE.55:3–2011

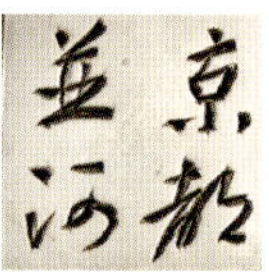

Plate. 28
V&A: FE.57:1–2011

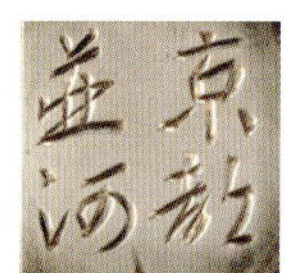

Plate. 29
V&A: FE.50:1–2011

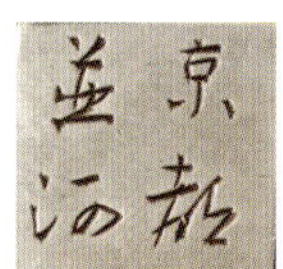

Plate. 31
V&A: FE.54:1+2–2011

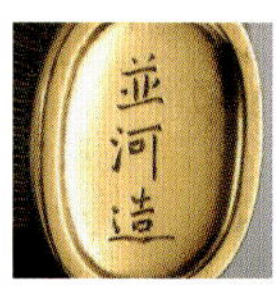

Plate. 33
V&A: FE.60:1+2–2011
V&A: FE.61:1+2–2011
V&A: FE.61:3+4–2011

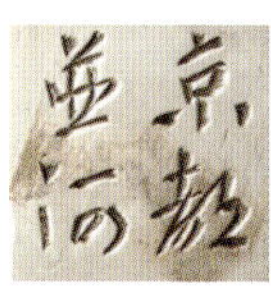

Plate. 34
V&A: FE.67–2011

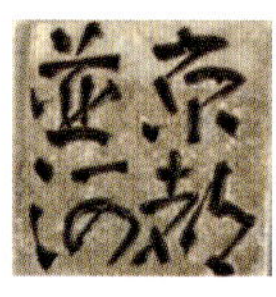

Plate. 35
V&A: FE.79–2011

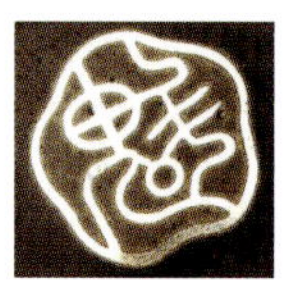

Plate. 36
V&A: FE.56:1–2011
V&A: FE.56:1–2011

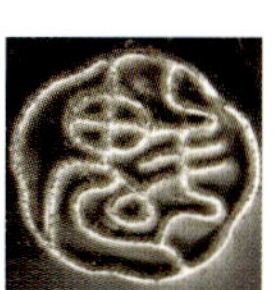

Plate. 37
V&A: FE.58:1-2011

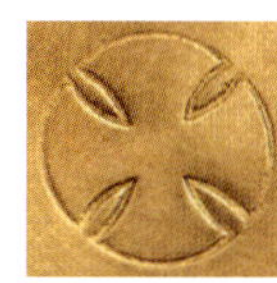

Plate 45
V&A: FE.71:1-2011

Plate. 38
V&A: FE.4:1-2011

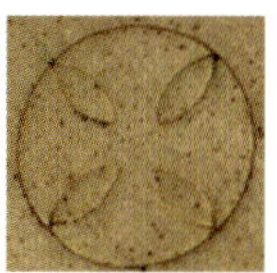

Plate. 46
V&A: FE.66:1-2011

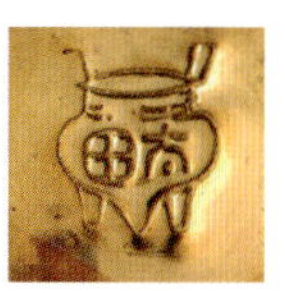

Plate. 39
V&A: FE.32:1-2011
V&A: FE.32:3-2011

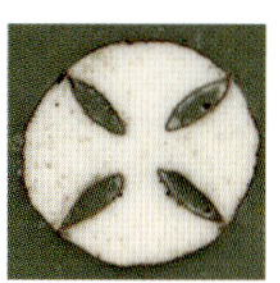

Plate. 48
V&A: FE.77:1-2011

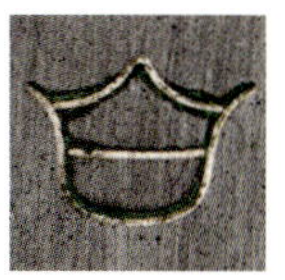

Plate. 40
V&A: FE.75:1-2011

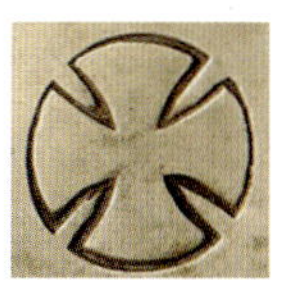

Plate. 51
V&A: FE.14:1-2011

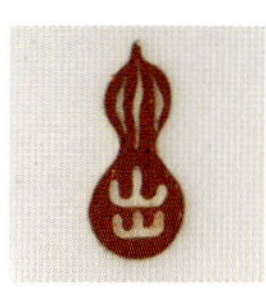

Plate. 41
V&A: FE.33:1+2-2011

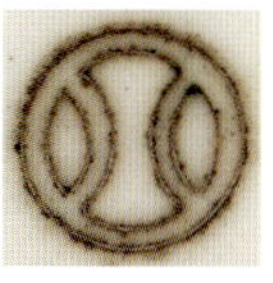

Plate. 52
V&A: FE.49:1-2011

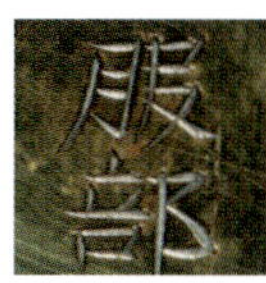

Plate. 42
V&A: FE.72:1+2-2011

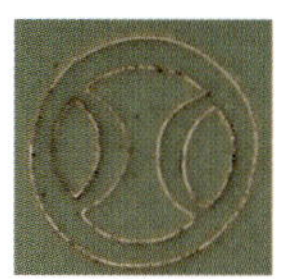

Plate. 54
V&A: FE.38:1-2011

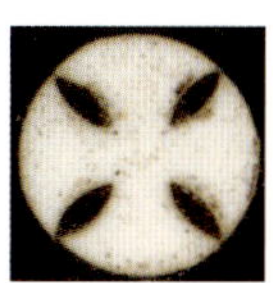

Plate. 44
V&A: FE.42:1-2011

Plate. 55
V&A: FE.74-2011

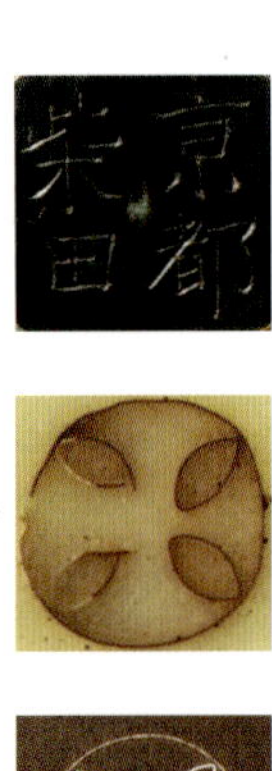

Plate. 57   V&A: M.68–1969

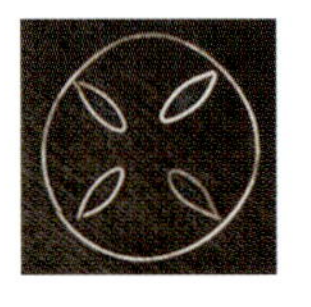

Plate. 69   V&A: FE.48:1-2011

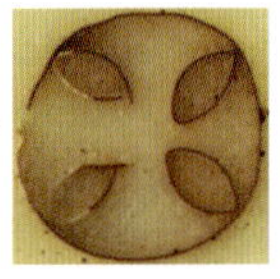

Plate. 61   V&A: FE.17:1-2011

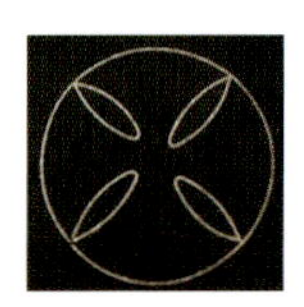

Plate. 70   V&A: FE.51:1-2011

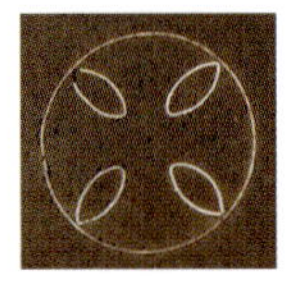

Plate. 62   V&A: FE.20:1-2011
             V&A: FE.20:3-2011

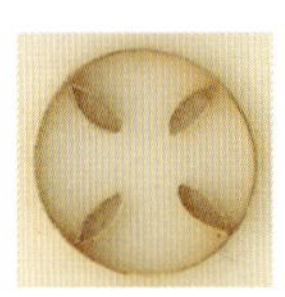

Plate. 71   V&A: FE.52:1-2011

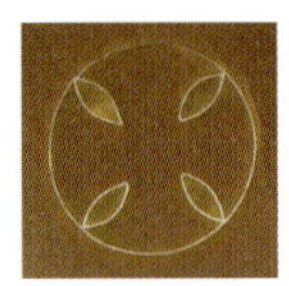

Plate. 64   V&A: FE.37:1-2011

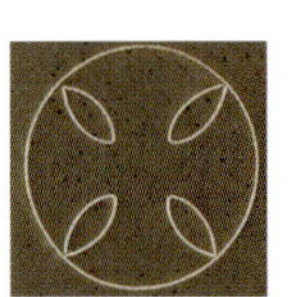

Plate. 72   V&A: FE.53:1-2011

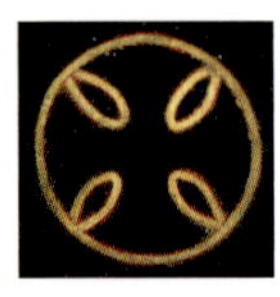

Plate. 65   V&A: FE.39:1-2011

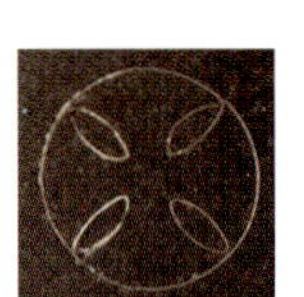

Plate. 73   V&A: FE.65:1-2011

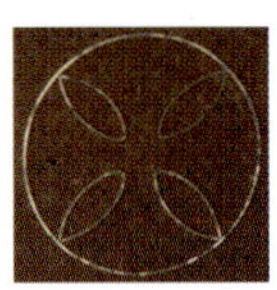

Plate. 66   V&A: FE.69:1-2011

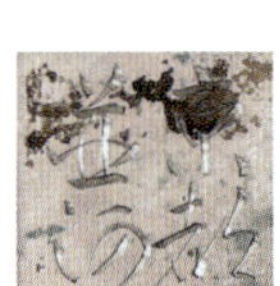

Plate. 88   V&A: M.73–1969

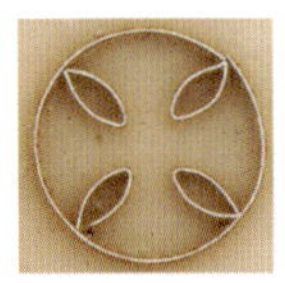

Plate. 68   V&A: FE.46:1-2011